A HISTORY
MUSIC OF BRISTOL

IN 100 OBJECTS

Edited by Wendy Wilby

This little book of resources is dedicated to
my husband, Phil, who has been a constant
support and a long-suffering companion.

First published in 2013 by Redcliffe Press Ltd.,
81g Pembroke Road, Bristol BS8 3EA

www.redcliffepress.co.uk
info@redcliffepress.co.uk

© the contributors

ISBN 978-1-908326-40-9

British Library Cataloguing-in-Publication Data
A catalogue record for this book is available from the British Library

Design and typesetting by Stephen Morris stephen-morris.co.uk
Arial 9.5 pt / 10.4 leading
Printed and bound by Short Run Press Ltd, Exeter

Contents

Foreword

Towards the end of the sixteenth century, the composer William Byrd wrote a Preface to his Psalms, Sonnets and Songs. It was his argument 'to perswade every one to learn to sing'. Singing, said the master, is easily taught and quickly learned and it is good for you:

> It doth strengthen all the parts of the brest and doth open the pipes

Furthermore, singing is glorious:

> There is not any Musicke of Instruments whatsoever, comparable to that which is made of the voices of Men, where those voices are good, and the same well sorted and ordered

Here, in what was St Augustine's Abbey, and is now Bristol Cathedral, singing (and a lot more music besides) has always been at the heart of what we do and it has always been essential that this music should be 'well sorted and ordered'. Cathedral music is a community event; it builds and expresses our relationships with one another. Of course, we take delight in the fact that our music is beautiful and attracts people into the building, but we value it most because, when we arrive here, music helps us feel that we belong to one another and to God.

So, it is a privilege to introduce Canon Wilby's book, a celebration not only of our music, but a reflection of our common life. It is a good book to carry around with you as you visit or to dip into later, as you explore a rich heritage that is still very much alive.

With Canon Wilby, I would like to thank all those who have helped her bring the project to completion; this book is, indeed, another community endeavour. We are also both deeply grateful to the Friends of Bristol Cathedral for the support that saw the book through production. In a Foreword, though, I can strike a more personal note and thank Canon Wilby for her part in sustaining the story of our music as our Precentor and then telling the story here with verve and delight. Here, too, things are 'well sorted and ordered' and, as William Byrd would have us remember, a thing well done gives honour to God.

David Hoyle
Dean of Bristol

Introduction

❀

England's many impressive cathedrals and parish churches should never become mere memorials and museums. They are testimonies to the living faith and God-given grace that can be found in countless men and women from centuries gone by to present times. Bristol Cathedral is one such building – we who love it have found it to be so.

The Cathedral is set in a vibrant city, and we have discovered hidden treasure there in a place which has faithfully resounded with the 'psalms, hymns and spiritual songs' offered to God by his people. This outstanding and unending music began with the chanting of the Augustinian Canons in the twelfth century, and still echoes today with the chanting of our Cathedral Choir. This all calls, at the very least, for a small and easily digestible record of its history – a little book of resources designed to introduce, inform and stimulate. I hasten to add that it isn't in any way designed to be a comprehensive and academic historical study, but its intriguing format should be sufficient to encourage a closer look and kindle a further desire to listen to the music that is created within this fine building.

I owe the concept of the book to an initiative promoted by the BBC. In 2010 a joint project of BBC Radio 4 and the British Museum called 'A History of the World in 100 Objects' was launched. It consisted of 100 fascinating, stand-alone 15-minute broadcast presentations. Objects of ancient art, industry, technology and arms, all of which are in the British Museum's collections, were used as an introduction to aspects of human history. You could listen to one or 10 or all 100 broadcasts with equal satisfaction. What a splendid idea this was, and it caught the imagination of many, including myself.

I trust that *A History of the Music of Bristol Cathedral in 100 Objects* will serve the same function. However, many of the 'objects' themselves are not inanimate. They include living, breathing human beings who have contributed to this resonant witness to God. There are also objects of wood and stone, manuscripts, musical instruments, old programmes and many more fascinating memorabilia – all captured in the excellent photography of Darren Bell (DB). I am so very grateful to him for his contributions, as I am, of course, to the many colleagues, musicians and local historians who have all been generous enough to take on one or more 'objects' and who have engaged our interest in many ways with their expertise and passion. Serving on the Chapter of the Cathedral as Canon Precentor (the priest who is concerned primarily with music and liturgy) has brought me into contact with this band of people, and together we continue to contribute our own metaphorical 'stones' to this unfolding and developing spiritual edifice called Bristol Cathedral in the time that is given to us. To work collaboratively on this project has felt exactly the correct way to proceed.

St Augustine of Hippo (354-430), whose Rule was followed by the Canons of the Abbey, spoke passionately of God's 'beauty so ancient and so new'. That same fascination with beauty extended to music, for he taught also that 'to sing once is to pray twice' – inspirational words surely that apply to all choral church music. Almost two centuries later these further wise words of Pope Gregory 'the Great' were written in a letter to St Augustine of Canterbury, another significant saint for us here in Bristol. He wrote: 'Things are not to be loved for places' sake, but the places for the sake of the good things in them.'

These good things I present to you for what they are – 'testimonies to the living faith and God-given grace that can be found in countless men and women from centuries gone by and in present times'.

Wendy Wilby, Canon Precentor
Bristol Cathedral,
Ash Wednesday, 13 February 2013

St Augustine's Abbey

THIRTEENTH-CENTURY PSALTER

The 150 Psalms in the Old Testament have for many centuries been the backbone for the Divine Office of the Christian Church. The recitation or chanting of them in plainsong occupied much of the liturgy, being interspersed with other scriptural passages and prayers. In monastic communities stretching back in time, the purpose of the Divine Office was (and still is) to sanctify the day and all human activity. The round of worship began with Matins (c. 2 am) to be followed by Lauds, Prime (6 am), Terce (9 am), Sext (noon), None (3 pm), Vespers (6 pm) and Compline (7 pm). During the Daily Mass (Eucharist) there would also be psalmody appropriate for the day recited between the readings from the scriptures.

This pattern of prayerful worship was observed in the Augustinian Abbey at Bristol, which would be dissolved at Henry VIII's sixteenth-century Reformation before becoming Bristol Cathedral. The Reformation made no difference to this tradition. Archbishop Cranmer rearranged the eight offices so as to become two (Matins and Evensong), during which the entire psalter was recited each month, alongside the reading of the New Testament every six months and the Old Testament once a year. Whereas the medieval arrangement broke up the material into smaller fragments, the Anglican Reformation soaked the worshipper in extensive recitation and readings. The liturgical reforms enshrined in Common Worship have reverted in part to the more selective approach as well as to the restoration of Compline as a separate office.

Of course, many manuscripts were lost as Henry VIII's officials swept by in their asset stripping. Medieval psalters were written on parchment and these were often recycled to serve as book covers, or their surfaces were scraped off so that they could be used for other purposes. One such psalter from the 1200s – shown here – seems to have come originally from St Augustine's Abbey before it became a cathedral. It later found its way by a circuitous route to Křivoklát Castle in Prague, where it now belongs to the Czech Republic; its details were published in 1972.*

This psalter features a calendar of festivals for each month, alongside representations of the labours appropriate for each period. Indeed, there are major illustrations throughout. Christmas scenes are portrayed in detail, followed by the Passion. The post-Resurrection scenes have not survived. Some of these images reflect English needlework and no doubt also wall paintings of the era, which regrettably have not survived in Bristol. The Henrician officials have removed references to the festivals for St Thomas Becket from this psalter – Henry disliked Becket's opposition to King Henry II and had his shrine at Canterbury desecrated, too. Other, locally important, commemorations remain in the psalter. These include the festival day of St Wulfstan, the Anglo-Saxon Bishop of Worcester (pre-Reformation Bristol was part of the Worcester Diocese), and that of St Brandon (or Brendan), remembered on Brandon Hill in Bristol. Naturally for an Augustinian abbey, the festivals of both Augustines, one of Canterbury and the other of Hippo, are included.

Psalms, then, were used from the day the Abbey was founded in 1140. This thirteenth-century psalter connects our present use with the Augustinian Canons who prayed with them centuries before.

*Full details are in 'The English Psalter in the Library of Křivoklát Castle' by Josef Krása, *Umění* [journal] vol. XX, Prague, 1972.

Coronation of the Virgin/Angelic Musicians from the
Křivoklát Psalter ©Stuart Whatling 2005

FOURTEENTH-CENTURY TEMPORALE

One of the oldest, and certainly most beautiful, items in the archives of Bristol Cathedral, which are kept at Bristol Record Office, is the book containing portions of a 'Temporale', created some time between 1350 and 1380.

The Temporale is the medieval service book containing words and music sung during services when the Cathedral was an Augustinian abbey. It is arranged according to the Church's liturgical year, hence use of the Latin word *tempora*, meaning over time or across the seasons, and would have had a companion volume – the 'Sanctorale' – containing music for the special services on saints' days. One can imagine the monks of St Augustine's Abbey congregated around the altar steps, singing together from these large pages of music.

Almost as fascinating as the book itself, is the story of how the segments from this Temporale came to be in the Cathedral's collection. In 1917, the Bishop of Bristol, George Forrest Browne, recorded how he bought a bundle of 'dirty and ragged old parchments … on the chance of their proving to have some interest when straightened out and cleared of dust and dirt'. From other markings on the parchment, it was evident to the Bishop that a chapter clerk had used the parchment as wrappers for Cathedral accounts for the years after 1557.

Following the dissolution of St Augustine's Abbey in 1539, King Henry VIII founded the Diocese and Bishopric of Bristol and the Abbey Church became the new Cathedral. However, although the old Abbey service books were no longer needed, the tough durability of parchment lent itself well to reuse and, in this case, was recycled as the covers of the Cathedral's accounts. What happened to the pieces of this Temporale in the intervening years, and how they came to be offered for sale to Bishop Browne, is difficult to say. The Bishop himself, who undertook a great deal of research as to their origins and was responsible for reordering and rebinding

Fragment of the Temporale. By kind permission of Bristol Record Office

them into one volume, speculated that

> the parcels [of accounts] had been tossed out at the burning of
> the bishop's palace in the [Bristol] riots of 1831 and a few of them
> had been carried off by some chance passer-by as a memento
> of the very formidable riots.

The Temporale has been kindly lent by Bristol Cathedral to M
Shed, Bristol's harbourside local-history museum, where it can
currently be seen on display.

THE MERMAID AND THE MONK

With its four-line stave, rather than five, and no time signature, clef
or bar lines, the musical notation of the Temporale appears strange

to our eyes today, unaccustomed as we are to the conventions of fourteenth-century musical notation. The music, known as 'sequences', was chanted plainsong, with the Latin scripture written in red voiced by the celebrant, and the texts in black sung in unison by the monks gathered around him.

Whilst this kind of music is now not heard quite so much, superseded as it has been by the use of harmony during the intervening centuries, the visual immediacy of the illuminated letters remains very much in the present. There is a wonderful, joyful sense of vitality and humour in the way that the scribes have carefully and expertly illuminated the texts, which really brings the pages to life. For example, in this rather unclear picture, as Bishop Browne noted, the mermaid (used to illustrate the 'D' of *Domine memorabor*), rather than holding a mirror and comb, is depicted as if having just shot an arrow across the page. On the facing page in the Temporale, a tonsured monk, as if defending himself against the lusty mermaid, is seen brandishing his weapon, perhaps a strigil, as though threatening to scrape off her seductive scales.

Illuminated letters from the Temporale. By kind permission of Bristol Record Office

4

TE DEUM LAUDAMUS

The 'Te Deum Laudamus' ('We praise you, O God') is one of those glorious hymns of praise that the Church seems to have sung from time immemorial. Its origins probably reach right back to the fourth century, and yet the hymn is still sung on high days and holidays in the Cathedral to this very day. Certainly the Augustinian Canons would have chanted it many times whilst the Abbey was in existence. It would have been sung regularly outside of the penitential seasons either after Mass or the Divine Office, or even as a separate religious ceremony to mark an event of importance. We have one such event recorded in the Episcopal register of Worcester. It describes the election in 1352 of William Coke, the Sub-Prior, as Abbot at Bristol. One can only imagine the excitement and anticipation associated with the occasion. All 17 Canons had assembled in the chapter house. This was the room set aside for meetings of the Augustinian community. In Bristol's case we are talking about a building that is one of the finest examples of Norman architecture in the world, completed in 1165. The Canons were gathering for the election and the result most certainly wasn't going to be a foregone conclusion. Nine voted for William Coke and eight for various other candidates. The Prior, Robert de Syde, announced the result:

> Whereupon, all having approved of the election, they raised the said William in their hands from the ground and carried him to the high altar, singing Te Deum Laudamus, and laid him upon the same altar, as is the custom.

It is interesting to note that in 2010 the current Cathedral community gathered in the same chapter house to hear the Bishop of Bristol make the announcement about the appointment of a new Dean. The expectation and eagerness was again huge, but sadly no 'Te Deum Laudamus' was sung and David Hoyle was not laid on the high altar!

Chapter House. (DB)

5

FIFTEENTH-CENTURY MISSAL OF THE VICTORINE CANONS

Walking through the cloisters towards the refectory, the casual observer will notice a sequence of stained-glass portraits over-looking the quadrangle. Although some of the glass is medieval, the greater majority of the panes is post-war and portrays significant moments in the Cathedral's long history. The last image is especially unusual and depicts a Roman soldier holding a windmill. This is St Victor, who was martyred for his faith and became a great influence on a number of leading medieval churchmen, notably St Ambrose of Milan, who died in 397. The Victorine order that consequently sprang up had its own Augustinian traditions, and these were introduced into the early days of the Abbey's liturgy. Bristol's Central Library now houses a few liturgical books which were arguably made at the Abbey, including a large Victorine missal and a more personal Book of Hours (owned by someone outside of the Abbey). They both date from the fifteenth century.

The larger volume is clearly an altar book and contains all the material needed for the celebration of the Latin Mass, along with its elaborate music. Illuminated capitals, including some in gold leaf, enliven this missal's text, and the plainsong settings are highly decorative. The scribe who made this book has also decorated the margins of the pages with floral motifs. Illustration work in this volume contains the intonation for the 'Kyrie' and a sequence of alternatives for the 'Gloria in Excelsis'. Interestingly, some of these melodies are still in use in the Cathedral's repertoire to this day. The final response, which is sung at daily Evensong, was also in use 500 years ago.

Perhaps the most interesting details of this rare volume are the manuscript additions, written in the margins of the text by the various users of the book. Occasional words are changed, and at some later stage certain passages have been scored through to conform with the political and religious edicts of the time. Perhaps most charmingly, the original monkish scribe has ended his work

Fifteenth-century Missal. By kind permission of Bristol Central Library

with a caricature of his tonsured self, depicted as a snail whose shell is apparently still writing!

6

LADY CHAPEL DEVOTION

We learn from 'Our Chapels' in The Friends of Bristol Cathedral Report and Notes of 1959-60 that the late thirteenth-century Eastern Lady Chapel, so beautifully and colourfully restored in 1935, was the domain of the Clerks of the Chapel, who were maintained by the Abbey Almoner. The clerks consisted of the Cantor and the Succentor and there were '6 boys of the chapel'. The boys were brought up on the premises, the Cantor often combining that office with that of 'Master of the Boys'. Interesting to note, of course, that the Cathedral nowadays combines the Organist's post with 'Master of the Choristers'. The Almoner himself in those days made sure that all were fed and clothed and, indeed, he brought all the boys up, paying for the washing of their clothes, the cutting of their hair and the mending of their heads when broken.

Alan Mould, in his excellent book *The English Chorister*, says that it has often been assumed that the almonry boys were there from the first to sing in the Lady Chapel. However, for some years, in most foundations, if not all, the boys were poor and simply receiving a free education as part of the charitable work of an abbey. They would serve as acolytes in the Masses, and it is only later that they were used as singers in the Lady Masses.

One piece of evidence concerning these singing boys comes from 1491/2, when St Augustine's Abbey paid 20d for accompanying a boy from St George's, Windsor, in order to add a trained chorister to the choir of Bristol's Lady Chapel. Later, in 1510, one Richard Bramston, alias Smyth (see entry no. 7), was spied back at his old haunt of Wells Cathedral (where he had been dismissed as Master of the Choristers). He was seen 'in privye and disguised apparel to have hadde away one of our best queresters, that is to say, Farre, and therewith takyn'. Even in those days it was never easy to recruit excellent boys into cathedral choirs!

Eastern Lady Chapel. (DB)

7

RICHARD BRAMSTON

In the early sixteenth century, the boys who sang in the choir of St Augustine's Abbey were taught at 'The Grammar School'. One master in charge of these boys was Richard Bramston. He was born in the latter part of the fifteenth century and became a Vicar Choral at Wells Cathedral in 1507. He was soon deputising for the Organist and Master of the Choristers. In 1508, however, he seems to have been on bad terms with the Chapter, who appointed another Vicar Choral in his place, whereupon he moved to St Augustine's Abbey as 'Master of the Boys'. As mentioned previously, in 1510 he was found attempting to poach a talented boy chorister from Wells in order to take him back to Bristol! In spite of that, two years later he was back at Wells as Organist and Master of the Choristers. There he remained for about 20 years before resigning, renouncing music and becoming a very prosperous businessman. He died in 1554.

Very little of Bramston's music has survived, but there are a few compositions still sung including his *Marie Virginis*. One piece for men's voices, edited by Richard Terry, is still published and worth a place in the repertoire. This is 'Recordare, Domine' ('Remember, O Lord [thy covenant]'), the words taken from the Introit of the Mass in Time of Pestilence, sometimes called the Mass for Avoiding Death (*pro morte evitanda*). Although part of the polyphonic repertoire, it is quite a 'chordal' piece, with decorations in the vocal line tending to come in the two tenor parts at cadences. It is in five sections, numbers two and three being verses for tenor one and bass two and tenor two and bass one respectively.

Antico Edition RCM107

John Catcott

Trium regum trinum munus

Richard Bramston

Marie virginis

Edited by Nick Sandon

Title page of compositions found in the Renaissance
Church Music section of *Antico Edition*

8

DISPUTES IN THE ABBEY

The Abbey's history appears to be consistently marked by financial embarrassment and a lack of governance, and these two factors led to internal dissension. Arguments, which lasted for some years, also began to break out between the Monastery and town. One such dispute involved the paying of taxes by musicians – often a problem to this very day, of course. During the rule of Abbot Somerset (1526–33), two choristers refused to pay the 'King's silver', and their goods were seized in lieu by the collectors. The consequence of that was that Abbot Somerset arrested the officers, whilst the Mayor imprisoned some Abbey servants. The Abbot, 'with a riotous company', attempted to force the prison but failed. The matter was finally referred to arbitration, and the result was that the choristers had to pay their taxes and the prisoners of both parties were released. In addition to this, the Mayor and Council had to attend services as usual. The Abbot and his successors, 'in token of submission for their contempt', had to meet or wait for them at the door of the grammar school at Froom Gate and accompany them into the Abbey. All this was to take place for the foreseeable future, upon each Easter Day in the afternoon and on the Monday in the morning. As you can imagine, this particular dictate did not bode well for future relations between Monastery/Cathedral and town.

Source used: 'Houses of Augustinian Canons: The Abbey of St Augustine, Bristol', in *A History of the County of Gloucester*, vol. II, 1907.

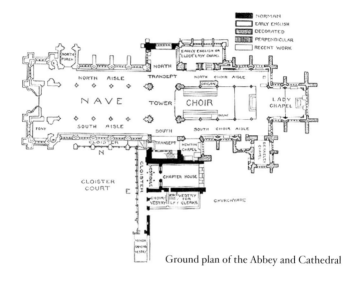

Ground plan of the Abbey and Cathedral

Renatus Harris on Choir Screen. By permission of Bristol Cathedral (hung in the Song School)

Organs

RENATUS HARRIS, 1682

Organs of a very primitive type were in use in nearly all the abbeys and cathedrals of England in the fourteenth century, and probably the Abbey of St Augustine (later to become Bristol Cathedral) was no exception.

The first actual record of an organ in this building occurs in *Newland's Roll*, a register of events in the Abbey's history, compiled by John de Newland (known as Nailheart), whose magnificent tomb can be seen in the Eastern Lady Chapel of the Cathedral. The original is lost, but a copy exists at Berkeley Castle. An entry in the *Roll* refers to Newland, who died in 1515, being 'beried in the south side of our Lady Chapell in the arch there by the dore going into the loft going to the organs'. This original screen probably stood at the entrance to the Eastern Lady Chapel.

In 1542 the Abbey became the Cathedral Church. Between 1542 and 1547 a stone screen was erected connecting the pillars that now face and back the Bishop's throne, and the organ was probably placed on this. In 1629 a new organ was built, and paid for by voluntary contributions, and it seems possible that this was one of the few organs that survived the Commonwealth unscathed, since it was claimed still to be in use some 20 years after the Restoration.

What is certain is that, in 1682, the Dean and Chapter commissioned a new 'fair great organ' from the distinguished organ builder Renatus Harris. Harris, together with his arch rival Bernard 'Father' Smith, dominated English organ building during the late seventeenth and early eighteenth century and built new organs in many other cathedrals, including Salisbury, Worcester and Winchester. At Bristol he provided a substantial instrument of 19 stops. This organ, which was placed on the screen, was completed in 1685, the year in which Bach and Handel were born. The two bays, as seen today, side by side, were originally the west and east fronts of the screen organ; the front pipes also date from 1685. The case (of which the western bay in particular is a magnificent example of seventeenth-century carving) was somewhat mutilated when it was moved from the screen in 1860.

Renatus Harris's organ had three keyboards: Great, Echo (the forerunner of the Swell) and Choir. The main development was the Great Organ, with a full compass and 12 stops. Several of the Great stops were borrowed, by a clever but erratic system that Harris favoured, to be playable on the Choir keyboard, which had no pipes of its own. The third keyboard was an Echo section of short compass, the pipes enclosed inside a simple box in the style typical of the time. There were no pedal keys.

Very little of this organ, save the displaced cases with their display pipes, remains today in the magnificent 1907 Walker instrument which graces the choir of our Cathedral Church.

WALKER REBUILD, 1907

Although the Cathedral organ had been rebuilt in 1860 by Vowles, it was still rather old-fashioned even at that time. The manuals had different compasses and the pedal department was very limited. With the building of the new nave in the 1870s, the organ was no longer adequate to serve a building that had doubled in length. When the choir area of the Cathedral was reordered in 1894-5, it was hoped that the organ could be rebuilt, but money could not be found and the project was abandoned.

In 1901, Hubert Hunt was appointed Organist, and he began to set in motion plans for the complete modernisation of the organ. Thanks largely to a generous donation from Mr H.O. Wills, by 1906

Walker rebuild. (DB)

it was possible for the work to be carried out. The organ builders selected were J.W. Walker & Sons, who had recently rebuilt the organs in York Minster and Rochester Cathedral. Surviving correspondence from the local press shows that some Bristol citizens were rather indignant that a local firm had not been selected for the project, and others (such as a correspondent calling himself 'Music v. Noise') were put out that the organ was to be enlarged at all. The responses of Hubert Hunt (also printed in the local press) to these criticisms were extremely skilful. In his last paragraph he would usually tell the correspondent that, of course, they were really in agreement and exactly why they should donate money to the organ fund. One wonders whether he could have made a career in diplomacy or law!

The work carried out produced what was almost a new organ. The mechanism was entirely new, as was much of the pipework.

There were now 60 stops, 26 of which were retained from the previous organ, including the 1,685 case pipes. The cases originally faced east and west on the choir (or quire) screen, until 1860. In that year the screen was removed and the organ rebuilt in the second bay on the north side of the choir (the former western case being wedged against the wall of the North Choir aisle). In the Walker rebuild, the cases were stood side by side, where they remain to this day.

The instruments mentioned above in York and Rochester have since been rebuilt many times, quite radically, and no longer resemble the instruments that Walker built prior to the Bristol one. This makes the organ of Bristol Cathedral unique and special, as it is the only surviving cathedral organ of the period built by Walker. Although unmistakably English in tone, it is nevertheless different in character from the instruments of more familiar builders such as Willis or Harrison. Its rather dark-hued sound has led to various descriptions in print such as 'Bournville chocolate character' and 'like a good pint of Younger's tartan'! More seriously, perhaps the 1962 article in *The Organ* magazine by Laurence Elvin sums it up: 'It is the creation of artists in voicing and tonal finishing, for it possesses an air of elegance throughout, each stop and each department being a model of tonal balance.'

What is most remarkable about the organ is its ability to make so many different schools and styles of music sound good, from early music (which we play nowadays in a totally different way to how it would have been played when this organ was built) to modern music written by composers who weren't even born when the organ was built. It stands as the last and finest of the best period of the English Romantic organ.

ORGAN RESTORATION, 1990

Some minor repairs and alterations were made to the organ in 1947 and 1970. Remarkably, the organ escaped the fashions of the 1960s and '70s, which saw many organs of similar age altered unsympathetically, but by around 1980, it was becoming clear that the organ needed major attention. It finally received a full restoration in 1989–90, carried out by N.P. Mander with Nicolas Kynaston as consultant. This restoration cost approximately £250,000, provided through the generosity of Bristol Cathedral Trust. It pursued the challenging course of retaining and restoring the 1907 mechanism, rather than converting it into a more modern, partly electric, operating system. This mechanism, although part of the ethos of the 1907 organ, is a particularly awkward design and very vulnerable to climate and humidity changes, and it was a Herculean task to restore it. At the same time, the opportunity was taken to add five more stops to the organ, although two of these were reinstated stops that had been removed in 1947 and 1970 – and with hindsight were wanted back! Also, the 'playing aids' of the organ console were increased and converted into a more modern operating system. This meant that the organist no longer had to crawl under the organ to set things up for playing, so this development came as a welcome relief!

The casework was cleaned, and the previous solid panels at the bottom of the case were replaced by wooden grilles designed by the Cathedral architect, Alan Rome – the pipes behind the casework had previously struggled to be heard. At the same time several wooden urns surviving from the original case, but removed when it was rearranged in the aisle, were attached to the northeastern corner of the case on wooden brackets.

Repair to some of the leatherwork was excluded from the 1990 restoration due to cost, and this work was carried out by Cawston Organs in 2004. At the same time, the console 'playing aids' were further increased, the mechanism was given a further service, and a few other minor repairs were undertaken. In 2009, the 'percussion section' (the very noisy operating mechanism) of one department was attended to, in order that listeners sitting in the choir area could actually hear the notes in very soft music.

And so it continues year by year. There is no doubt that pipe organs 'eat money' in cathedrals and churches, and it is proving a real battle to convince congregations and benefactors that these mighty beasts are worthy to be kept alive. Fortunately for us, the organ of Bristol Cathedral is an outstanding specimen. We hope that, at its next restoration, people will look favourably upon the project, to ensure that future generations can continue to enjoy this magnificent instrument.

Wooden grilles replaced solid panels. (DB)

THE EASTERN LADY CHAPEL CHAMBER ORGAN

This small organ was built in 1956, but its history goes back much further. The case was first built in 1786 to house the Choir manual of the Cathedral organ. It was bracketed out behind the organist's seat when the organ was on the screen across the choir. The instrument was known as a 'chair-organ' because, when such organs were originally built, the organist had to turn round on his seat to play the organ behind him. This case was removed in 1860, sold by the Cathedral and converted into a domestic bookcase which was for many years in use at Deerhurst Priory, Clifton Down. It was discovered by Mr H.P. Chadwyck-Healey, who in 1956 presented it to the Cathedral and paid for a new organ to be built inside it, in memory of the late Sir Sydney Nicholson (the founder of what is now the Royal School of Church Music), who had died in 1947. Mr R.H. Brentall designed the reordering of the case. The organ was built by Harrison and Harrison and designed by them in conjunction with Clifford Harker, the Cathedral Organist of the time. The stoplist is very closely related to the Choir manual that the case housed in the eighteenth century – four out of five stops are the same.

Chamber organ. (DB)

OTHER CHAMBER ORGANS

The Cathedral was delighted to welcome, in the summer of 2013, a new four-stop continuo chamber organ built by Kenneth Tickell. It is housed in the choir and can be used for those Choral Evensongs during which the choir sings early music. It has been paid for by a donation in memory of Ron Apperley, who was a member of the congregation and an avid supporter of the music of the Cathedral.

In the redundant Bristol church of St Nicholas, lately a museum but now an office for architects, rests a beautiful chamber organ which lies totally dormant. It is the Cathedral's hope that this instrument, made by Sarah Green, will eventually make its way to the Eastern Lady Chapel and spring to musical life once more. Sarah was the wife of Samuel Green. He was the great grandson, on his mother's side, of Renatus Harris, who was a master organ maker in England in the late seventeenth and early eighteenth centuries. Harris built the large pipe organ in Bristol Cathedral (see entry number 9).

After an organ-building apprenticeship, Samuel Green started his own business in 1772 and became a top-ranking builder for the rest of his life. During this time he constructed or rebuilt over 60 organs, including those for Canterbury and Wells cathedrals. George III especially liked the 'sweetness and tone' of Green's organs and appointed him royal organ builder. Despite this accolade, he died penniless in 1796, aged 56. Sarah, his wife, took over his business for a short time in partnership with Benjamin Blythe, who had been her husband's foreman.

The beautiful chamber organ in the photograph bears a wooden nameplate which includes 'by Appointment to His Majesty George III' and is dated 1797, so Sarah may have simply just completed the job. There is only one other surviving organ credited to her, at St Michael's Parish Church at Baddesley, Clinton, in Warwickshire.

This instrument was found in a girl's school in Plymouth, in a

Chamber organs built by Sarah Green, *left*, and by Kenneth Tickell, *right*

very dilapidated state, during the early 1970s and was brought to Bristol and placed in the St Nicholas Museum. It was restored to its former beauty by Noel Mander, in 1975. Now fitted with an electric blower, the instrument is still playable, demonstrating the soft, mellifluous tones for which the Green organs were noted.

We continue to hope that it will have a new home in the Eastern Lady Chapel of Bristol Cathedral – a very fitting place to be, so close to its distant cousin, the Renatus Harris/Walker pipe organ.

ORGAN BUILDERS ADJACENT TO THE CATHEDRAL

After the 1685 installation of the large, three-manual organ by Renatus Harris, the Cathedral authorities consistently sought to preserve their original instrument, whilst working to develop and expand it as musical tastes evolved. Central to this policy was the custodianship of local specialists who operated from premises originally situated in College Street, later moving to the premises of the Vowles's company in St James's Square. Brice Seede registered his organ-building firm at No. 3 College Street in 1775, and the company built an enlarged choir organ for the Cathedral in 1780. The finely carved casework was later used in the chamber organ which has been housed in the Eastern Lady Chapel.

In 1792, under the ownership of Brice's son, Richard, the company expanded its operations and moved to No. 4 College Street, where it remained until 1801. Subsequent proprietors of this firm have included the two John Smiths (senior and junior) and Joseph Munday, who all contributed to the creation of an independent pedal division. Although common to organs in northern Europe, separate pipework for use by the player's feet was still a novelty in England, and Bristol was one of the pioneers of a musical technique which has opened the door to an essential European repertoire for the instrument by J.S. Bach and others.

In Edward Hodges' illuminating diary of 1836, a description of Smith the Younger's new organ for Bristol's St Stephen's Church – 'embodying all the latest improvements' – is given, as well as a description of the revolutionary instrument at St James's Church. There was a triple swell box, and three sets of Venetian blinds, so called. Very grand effects were possible, if judiciously managed. The pedal keys were of iron, and first introduced in this organ. It was the first CCC pedal made in England. The same plans were adopted in Trinity Church, New York.

The final owner of the company was Munday's son-in-law, W.G. Vowles, who was in charge of the business by 1860, when the

Bristol Cathedral organ was rebuilt and moved. At its height, in 1871, the firm employed 27 men, 3 apprentices and 4 boys. Vowles was very disheartened that the Chapter did not employ them again in 1907 when the Cathedral organ was rebuilt once more. William Vowles died in 1912.

THE CATHEDRAL ORGAN.

SIR,—In your paragraph in to-day's issue referring to the Cathedral organ there is one passage which kindly allow me to correct. This is "for it is gradually collapsing."

When, in 1860, the organ was removed from the screen to nearly its present position, it was entirely re-built as regards its main portions, the pipes and case being repaired and retained. The work was done thoroughly and strongly. The instrument, as far as its capability for continued usefulness is concerned, is as good now as then, and it is not in accordance with facts to say it is collapsing.

That it requires modernising and enlargement, I am quite aware, and a scheme for so doing was submitted by myself, at request, at the time of the last restoration of the Cathedral. The matter, however, dropped for want of funds and other causes. I may add, that I have not been consulted in the present business, or even asked for an estimate, although my predecessors and myself have been connected with the Cathedral for 80 years.

Yours truly,
W. G. VOWLES.

3, St. James's Square, Bristol.

Organists

Organists Past and Present

ORGANISTS

Thomas Denny (Senny)*	1542
Humphrey Walley	1546
Walter Glesson	1552
John Farrant	1570
Anthony Pryn	1571
Elway Bevin	1589
Edward Gibbons	1637
Arthur Phillips	1638
Thomas Deane	1640
Paul Heath	1680
Joseph Gibson	1687
Stephen Jeffries	1701
Nathaniel Priest	1724
James Morley	1734
George Coombes	1756
Edward Higgins	1759
George Coombes (reappointed)	
	1765
Edward Rooke	1769
Samuel Mineard	1773
Richard Langdon	1778
Rice Wasbrough	1781
Joseph Kemp	1802
John Wasbrough	1807
John Davis Corfe	1825
George Riseley	1876

Percy Buck	1899
Hubert Hunt	1901
Alwyn Surplice	1946
Clifford Harker	1949
Malcolm Archer	1983
Christopher Brayne	1990
Mark Lee	1998-

Denny was the organist appointed at the Reformation (according to the statutes of Henry VIII's Foundation, dated 4 June 1542), at a salary of 10s per annum.

ASSISTANT ORGANISTS

John Barrett	1858
George Riseley	1862
Albert Edward New	1876
J.H. Fulford	1888
Arthur S. Warrell	1902
Geoffrey Leonard Mendham	
	1920
Michael Dyer	1959
John Jenkins	1977
Martin Schellenberg	1980
Anthony Pinel	1986
Claire Hobbs	1989
Ian Ball	1992
David Hobourn	1996
Paul Walton	2001-

JOHN FARRANT, 1570-71

Under the reign of the Tudor monarchs, when written records and musical scores were all too often a rarity, and when compositions were circulated in individual part-books, it is not surprising that many fine pieces have been lost. Equally, musicians often passed on their posts to close relatives in these early times, and so an understandable confusion persists surrounding the identity of many composers.

John Farrant is a good case in point. He is supposed to have been a son of Richard Farrant, who sang at the Chapel Royal until 1564 and who was particularly associated with the Court at Windsor, where he took a leading role in the 'choirboy's theatricals' and the formation of the Blackfriars Theatre. Certainly we do know that an organist called John Farrant took duty for one year at Bristol Cathedral, between 1570 and 1571, and we may assume, although we cannot be totally sure, that he is the same man who also served at Hereford and Salisbury cathedrals and at London's Christ Church, Newgate Street. It is quite possible that all the above appointments were held in turn by the same person. The sands of time have obscured true identities, but we can be pleased to note that they have left us some fine music to remember them by.

The most famous anthem to bear the family name is 'Lord for Thy tender mercies' sake', which still finds a place on cathedral

music lists. Although much loved, it is perhaps the work of Richard, although some have ascribed it to the pen of John Hilton. However, a fine Service in D Minor is arguably the composition of John Farrant, and one that Bristol may proudly claim as giving a smidgeon of reflected glory.

ELWAY BEVIN, 1589-1637

Much of the detail concerning Bevin's tenure as Cathedral Organist was destroyed with the burning of the Cathedral library during the Reform Riots in 1831. However, we do know that he was born in Wales, and that he was probably a pupil of Thomas Tallis. He served briefly at Wells Cathedral and was appointed to Bristol as Master of the Choristers and subsequently as Organist in 1589. He is now remembered for his 'Dorian' Service, which has the rare distinction of having been included in William Boyce's famous eighteenth-century collection of *Cathedral Music* (see entry no. 30). This groundbreaking collection, begun by Maurice Greene and finally published in 1773, offered subscribers the very first opportunity to study many works by Byrd, Tallis and their Tudor contemporaries. Bevin's biography also appears in Sir John Hawkins's seminal 'Musical History' (*General History of the Science and Practice of Music*, five volumes, 1776). In addition to his Cathedral duties in Bristol, Bevin (sometimes spelt Bevan) became a member of the Chapel Royal in 1605.

For all church musicians, these were turbulent times, and Anthony Wood, in a source now lost in the 1831 fire, asserts that Bevin lost both his Cathedral and Royal positions upon accusations of Romanism. The last surviving reference to his career appears in remarks from one of Archbishop Laud's diocese 'visitations' of 1634, where he is described as a 'verie old man'.

It seems possible that Bevin also served at the Cathedral's neighbouring church, St Augustine-the-Less, during these years of difficulty. Certainly he attained a high reputation as an educa-

Magnificat in the Dorian Mode

Elway Bevin (Bristol)

(DB)

tionalist, and his teaching manual, a *Brief and Short Instruction in the Art of Musicke*, was published in 1631. A major work of instruction in the traditional art of composing counterpoint, it was dedicated to Bishop Goodman of Gloucester, and a copy survives in the Royal Library at Windsor. His setting of the English melody 'The Leaves Be Greene' (or 'Browning') is still a popular item with early-music ensembles.

18

EDWARD GIBBONS, 1637-8

It is indeed a treat to have a connection, however tenuous, with Orlando Gibbons, whose music is sung regularly at Choral Evensongs in the Cathedral. It appears that Orlando was born into a very musical family. As William Boyce said, he was 'born among the Muses and Musick'. His father and three of his brothers were musicians, and the brother we are concerned with here at Bristol is Edward Gibbons. Edward, the eldest surviving brother, was born in 1567/8 in Cambridge. Clearly he was a singer, a Lay Clerk, who eventually left Cambridge for Exeter Cathedral, where he served for some considerable time. Many have thought that he became a priest, but there is no written evidence for that. Indeed, Canon Edmund Fellowes, one of Bristol's own Precentors and a renowned scholar, has even questioned his appointment at Bristol as Organist in 1637 (see *Orlando Gibbons and His Family*, Edmund H. Fellowes, Oxford University Press, 1951).

Whatever is the truth of his employment, we do know that, in 1634, he became the subject of formal protest on the part of two of the lay vicars at Exeter, who, at Archbishop Laud's 'visitation', complained that there were four instead of six priest vicars, but that 'one of them was a leaman namely Mr Edward Gibbins…the fore named Mr Edward Gibbins doth not sitt in his place and read and singe at devine service tyme as the rest doth but once a quarter or ther about doth sitt in his place for two or three dayes but doth not usu-

Orlando Gibbons, brother of Edwar

ally do it as ye rest.'

One wonders whether this sort of complaint was enough to send him off to Bristol, where many have thought that he shared the organ bench with Elway Bevin.

PAUL HEATH, 1680-87

There are countless stories of drunkenness and debauchery in and around the cathedrals of England at this time. On one level, they make for amusing reading, but it all clearly springs from the paucity of payments to singing men and organists and the consequent lack of direction and sense of self-worth. One such character who fits the bill here is Cathedral Organist Paul Heath.

He 'debauched the vicars', allowing them to tipple in his house until they were 'very much overgone with liquors'. One was even found dead in the morning after carousing all night. As if this were not enough, Heath also rented rooms in his house to a barber who was accustomed to carry on with his trade on Sundays.

A typical barber's shop

The Bristol Record Office holds the actual Chapter Minute of 13 December 1682:

> It appearing to the Deane and Chapter that Paule Heath, Organist and Master of the Choristers, hath had severall admonitions for keeping a Disorderly Alehouse, Debauching the Choirmen and other disorders there, and neglecting the service of the Church: and beeing now Credibly Informed that the said Paule Heath doth still keep ill-order in his house, and hath suffered one Rouch, a barber, to trime in his house on the Lord's Day, commonly called Sunday … the said Deane and Chapter … did … order and Decree to remove, expell and dissmisse the said Paul Heath from his said office and place of Organist and Master of the Choristers.

In 1683, the usual salary is entered, but the Organist's name is not mentioned! This, along with the above order for dismissal, suggests strongly that he was no longer organist at that time. However, some doubt hangs over his years of tenure and several sources give his dates as 1680–87, which is why those dates have been chosen here … perhaps he managed to mend his ways?

JOHN DAVIS CORFE, 1825-76

There was, at one time in the Cathedral, a memorial window dedicated to the memory of John Davis Corfe, who was Organist for 51 years in the early part of the nineteenth century. He was appointed in the year that Beethoven wrote his last quartets and died in the year that Wagner opened the Bayreuth Theatre with the first performance of his 'Ring' cycle of operas. Although these were stirring times for the international development of music, Corfe's interests were primarily local. Indeed, such were the times in which he lived that he may be forgiven for appearing to be a musician whose lot was to react to external events rather than follow his own initiatives.

Name.	Abode.	When buried.	Age.	By whom the Ceremony was performed
George Gay No. 385.	Easton Place Easton Road	May 27	40 years	Nugent Wade Canon in Res.
John Davies Corfe Organist of this Cathedral Church from No. 386. 1825 to 1876.	31 Richmond Terrace Clifton	Jan. 21	yrs. 71.	C.S. Hey Precentor
James Bankly... Bellamy No. 387.	2. Shaftesbury Terrace S. Burton Bristol	Dec. 24.	yr. 37.	C.S. Hey Precentor

Cathedral burial register

He had been born in Salisbury in 1804 and was the musician in post during the riots of 1831. The loss of the Cathedral's music library is discussed elsewhere, but we can imagine that much of Corfe's time was spent rebuilding the repertoire of daily services which had been passed down from his predecessor John Wasbrough. With the formation of the Bristol Madrigal Society, he became its first conductor, and the tradition of a 'City Musician', whose main activities were concerned with the place of music within a greater social context, fits his tenure very well.

Within the city, these were years of optimism and much new building work was begun. In 1876, at the end of Corfe's long period of service, the new Colston Hall opened, and civic music making found a new and more worldly focus. In ecclesiastical circles, the Catholic pro-Cathedral (later to become Clifton Cathedral) opened in 1850, and at the Anglican Cathedral the Dean and Chapter had major building ambitions of their own. Construction work on G.E. Street's new nave began in 1868.

GEORGE RISELEY, 1876-99 (HIS DISPUTE WITH THE DEAN)

Amongst the Cathedral community there will inevitably, from time to time, be disagreements, disputes and dissent that will need to be resolved. And, bearing in mind the artistic temperament, it might not come as too much of a surprise to learn that the Cathedral records show a not inconsiderable share of these tensions emerging between the musicians, on the one hand, and the Chapter, on the other.

In 1895, tensions surfaced between the Organist, George Riseley, and the Precentor. Things eventually came to a head, and Riseley appealed to the Bishop against an order from the Dean and Chapter. This required him to fulfil his duties according to what they considered to be the terms of his appointment and 'admonished him as to the consequences of further disobedience'. The Chancellor of the Diocese, Judge Ellicott, acting for the Bishop, heard the appeal in the Cathedral's chapter house on 3 April. Riseley's defence relied on an informal agreement made between himself and Canon Girdlestone, who had since died, and which the Chapter had not been aware of until much later. But in any case, the Chapter argued, he had not even conformed to that agreement. Although those engaged in presenting the case for either side tried to keep their arguments focussed on the requirements of the role of Cathedral Organist, the reports from witnesses at the hearing revealed numerous instances of petty squabbling, musical differences, insults and other bad behaviour resulting from this clash of personalities. Ellicott deferred judgement until 27 May, when he dismissed Riseley's appeal. Riseley subsequently resigned his post, although, nevertheless, he was granted a pension by the Chapter.

Vacations.

The Chapter may probably require some modification in the matter of vacations. It will also require the Precentor to observe, from the 1st July next, the direction of our statutes, viz. :—The Precentor shall truly and impartially mark the absence from Divine service as well of the Dean and Canons as of all who serve in the choir.

Yours faithfully,

GILBERT ELLIOT.

To this Mr. Riseley replied :—

11, Charlotte-St., Park-St., Bristol, June 9th, 1885.

To the Very Rev. the Dean.

Rev. Sir,—I beg to acknowledge your letter of the 9th instant, *re* new scheme to be brought forward at the next Chapter meeting.

In the interest of the Cathedral I am ever ready to give my best efforts for the improvement of the services, *but only in accordance with the agreement made by Canon Girdlestone on behalf of the Dean and Chapter, and ratified by him, a copy of which I sent you on November 12th, 1884.*

Believe me, faithfully yours,

G. RISELEY.

ALFRED HERBERT BREWER, 1885 (ORGANIST FOR A FEW WEEKS)

Alfred Herbert Brewer's tenure at Bristol was extremely short – virtually non-existent! Elected Organist in September 1885, at the young age of 20, he became embroiled in a dispute between the Cathedral Chapter and the previous organist George Riseley. Eventually, Brewer sensibly gave way (after which Riseley resumed his Bristol post) and went on to become organist of St Michael's Church, Coventry a year later.

Fuller details of this little-known episode are given in Watkins Shaw's volume *The Succession of Organists* (Clarendon Press, 1991). The son of a Gloucester hotelier, Brewer had been a cathedral chorister there and a pupil of Thornbury-born C.H. Lloyd. He later joined the ranks of the many distinguished pupils of Sir Walter Parratt. These included Vaughan Williams, Harold Darke, John Ireland and Herbert Howells, along with other musicians whose influence was very strongly felt in Bristol. Both Percy Buck and Walford Davies were fellow students, and Brewer's return to Gloucester as organist in 1896 marked one of the most illustrious moments in the recent history of the Three Choirs Festival, where Brewer conducted many new works by Edward Elgar.

Now known mainly for his service music (in particular his Canticle settings in D and E flat), Brewer wrote music characterised by a workmanlike approach still much valued by choirs throughout the Anglican Church. Knighted in 1926, he stayed in Gloucester until his death in 1928.

Alfred Herbert Brewer. © National Portrait Gallery, London

PERCY BUCK, 1899-1901

Compared to the sterling service offered to the Cathedral by his successor, Buck's tenure was short, since he was called to serve as Head of Music at Harrow School within three years of his arrival in Bristol. By contrast, Hubert Hunt's 45-year career oversaw the installation of the Cathedral's mighty Walker organ in 1907 and brought a stability to the post in a time of great change. However, Buck has left us a rare survival, in the shape of his 1901 collection of five manuscript part-books, which offer a unique glimpse of the Cathedral's musical ambitions at this time.

Currently preserved in the Chapter Vestry Library, Buck's hand-written organ book also serves as a conductor's score, and 23 pieces are included. Of these, ten may be regarded as following an awakening interest in early music and include titles by Munday, Palestrina, Weelkes, Wilbye and Gibbons. Composers of the nineteenth century include S.S. Wesley, Mendelssohn, Molique and Parry. Most exceptionally, there are some compositions for men's voices only, including two rare examples by Henry Walford Davies. Of these, the setting of 'Father of Heaven', in six unaccompanied parts, deserves much wider recognition. Dated October 1896, it stands as a testament to Buck's time as a fellow pupil alongside Davies under Sir Walter Parratt. Other fellow pupils included Herbert Brewer, later of Gloucester Cathedral, Herbert Howells, composer, and Leopold Stowkowski, star conductor of Walt Disney's classic 'Fantasia'.

The book has been much used, and the contents page marks out nine pieces for special attention. These scores are meticulously edited for rehearsal and include notes to the conductor alongside extra phrasing and dynamics. The full score of R.L. Pearsall's mighty, four-movement setting 'I will cry unto God' is an especially well-prepared example, paying particular attention to the treble part, but also containing a hurried musical scribble – 'Altos Hurry!' – in the final fugue. Pearsall, who was born in Clifton

Percy Buck's signature in a hand-written organ book

in 1795, composed many of his most well-known pieces for the newly formed Bristol Madrigal Society (now the Bristol Chamber Choir).

24

HUBERT HUNT, 1901-45

As the nineteenth century drew to a close, it must have seemed that the tenure of Bristol organists had become disappointingly foreshortened. Percy Buck's time in Bristol lasted only two years, and Alfred Herbert Brewer's appointment was cut short before it had begun. How marked a contrast is the service offered by Hubert Hunt, whose time in Bristol began with the major rebuilding of the Cathedral's organ and encompassed the two World Wars. In combination with Clifford Harker, his near successor, they served both Cathedral and City as Organist for 80 years.

Son of Thomas Hunt, lately a Lay Clerk at Windsor, Hubert sang as a royal chorister until 1880 and then studied the organ in that famous company of pupils surrounding Sir Walter Parratt. Like so many of his contemporaries, he formed part of that generation of musical amateurs whose ability was beyond question, but whose qualifications were mainly honorary. His DMus was given by Lambeth Palace (a distinction which can still be recalled from the Middle Ages) and his FRCO was awarded *In Honoris Causa* in 1939.

In addition to his Cathedral work, Hunt was instrumental in forming a number of institutions that still foster the place of music within the community. The Bristol Music Club (Hunt was a keen violinist and chamber-music player), the Bristol Madrigal Choir (Hunt conducted this for 30 years) and the Bristol and District Organists' Association were all part of his vision for artistic endeavour in the wider sense.

Hunt's energy in redesigning the Cathedral organ and its inauguration in 1907 must be regarded as his major legacy and is the subject of a separate entry in these pages. However, his compositions also deserve a mention here. Although lacking the distinction of his fellow student colleagues, Walford Davies and Percy Buck, Hunt's music forms an interesting part of the musical and social fabric of his times. In particular, his 'Hymn of Reunion', written for the annual reunion of the Bristol Cathedral Old Choristers' Association,

A HYMN OF REUNION

Written for the
Annual Reunion
of the
Bristol Cathedral Old Choristers' Association

Words by
ARTHUR L. SALMON

Music by
HUBERT W. HUNT

is designed to unite the efforts of the present choir with a unison line of alumni from the past. In fact it has been sung in recent times, when the Old Choristers' Association was reformed in 2011. Stirring in style, it includes quotations from a pair of S.S. Wesley's lesser-known anthems. The closing lines of Arthur Solomon's text might well have served as an epitaph on Hunt's long and dedicated service:

> So may our lips and lives unite,
> A perfect gift to bring,
> And shine with the eternal Light,
> And live the love we sing.

Hubert Hunt's gravestone in the Cathedral garden (DB)

ALWYN SURPLICE, 1946-9

As the Cathedral Organist who was appointed to Bristol Cathedral immediately after the war years, Surplice's short tenure must have been a difficult one. He followed and preceded the epic innings of Hubert Hunt and Clifford Harker respectively. Equally, rather as may be observed about John Davis Corfe, whose appointment embraced a period of prodigious change in a variety of ways, Surplice's time must have been greatly affected by enormous amounts of rebuilding, both within the Cathedral building and in the city at large.

Nevertheless, before Surplice undertook a new challenge at Winchester Cathedral, where he stayed for the greater part of his career, he created some much-needed stability as he rebuilt the traditions of his predecessors. He reintegrated the Men and Boys' Choir into the *Opus Dei* of Cathedral life, and he brought back singers after their National Service years. In addition, as part of rebuilding close ties with the Cathedral School, he taught a number of well-known students, including David Chandler, President-elect of the Bristol and District Organists' Association. He wrote a number of excellent compositions, including the hymn tune 'Wessex', often sung to the words 'Brightest and best are the sons of the morning', and taught for many years at the Royal Academy of Music.

CLIFFORD HARKER, 1949-83

The legacy of Clifford Harker at Bristol Cathedral and indeed Bristol itself is huge. He is recalled with great affection by many former choristers and his influence still echoes around the Augustinian Abbey walls. Clifford followed St Augustine's motto: 'Pray as though everything depends upon God but work as though everything depends upon yourself.' These words appear on his memorial plaque in the Cathedral.

When he died on 2 November 1999 the following obituary was written by Tim Bullamore and it sums up his life and influence extremely well:

> Clifford Harker took over the console of Bristol Cathedral at a time of great change. Hubert Hunt had ruled the organ loft for most of the first half of this century but his successor, Alwyn Surplice, stayed for just three years before moving to Winchester. Between his appointment in 1949 and his retirement in 1983, Harker held firm to the musical and choral traditions of Bristol's great twelfth-century centre of worship, creating a force of stability for those who worshipped and sang there.

Harker was a champion of the West Country composer Sir Edward Elgar. His conducting of works such as 'The Apostles', 'The Kingdom' and 'Dream of Gerontius' was large and sweeping in style. After one performance of 'The Kingdom', the composer's daughter, Alice, who had been in the audience, wrote to congratulate him saying: 'It was just as he [Elgar] would have wished it.' Similarly, annual performances of Handel's 'Messiah' were grandiose and dramatic, albeit occasionally at the expense of some of the detail.

The son of a music critic on the *Newcastle Evening Chronicle*, Clifford Harker graduated from Durham University and studied at the Royal College of Music with Sir Malcolm Sargent and Ralph Vaughan Williams. During the Second World War he served with

'Clifford and his boys' in the Song School

the RAF in Cairo and was soon appointed Music Director of Music for All, an Egyptian organisation that promoted concerts. He founded a male voice choir, directed a choral society, conducted the Egyptian première of 'Messiah' in the old Cairo Cathedral and toured the Palestine Symphony Orchestra around the region. He said: 'I was one of the few people to be disappointed when the war ended.' On demobilisation, Harker became Organist at Rugby parish church and spent a brief but unhappy spell as Professor of Piano at Trinity College of Music in London.

After taking up his post at Bristol, Harker established a reputation as one of the foremost musicians in the region. His accompanying skills in works such as the Psalms – a matter of liturgy all too often forgotten or abandoned by today's Church –

were inspirational, and his ability to improvise from the organ loft was renowned.

He founded the Bristol Cathedral Special Choir in 1953 and became Music Director of the Bristol Choral Society in 1960 and the Bath Choral Society four years later. Although local to each other, all these choirs have their own distinct identity and Harker ensured that they continued to enjoy their separate voices. Even when seriously ill in the mid-1970s he refused to disappoint, conducting at least two performances of 'Messiah' in Bath Abbey sitting down.

During his tenure, Bristol Choral Society, which performs at the Colston Hall, had more than 200 members, a vocal force which suited the grand English choral tradition from which Harker came. He thrived on the Victorian and Edwardian classics but was not afraid to include repertoire by more modern composers such as Malcolm Williamson and Raymond Warren.

FINAL RESTING PLACES

Not content with long days spent in the Cathedral throughout the year, often over the duration of a long career, many organists choose to find their final resting place within the building where so much of their working life was spent. Rather like the much-married woman in the parable, those who have worked in a number of cathedrals may have to make a choice at the last judgement. When their place of burial isn't their final cathedral one may be left to muse upon the reason; Samuel Sebastian Wesley, for example, chose to return to Exeter, despite having died in Gloucester!

Of the 32 known and recorded Organists of Bristol Cathedral, of whom three are still alive, we can say for certain that six are buried in the Cathedral, either in the building itself or in the Cathedral garden. The list is as follows:

	appointed	died	buried
Edward Higgins	1759	1769	North Transept
Edward Rooke	1769	1773	North Transept
Rice Wasbrough	1781	1802	South Choir Aisle
John Wasbrough	1807	1825	South Choir Aisle
Hubert Hunt	1901	1945	Cathedral garden, brass plaque on door of organ loft
Clifford Harker	1949	1999	Ashes interred in Cathedral garden, brass plaques on door of organ loft and choir stalls north

(DB)

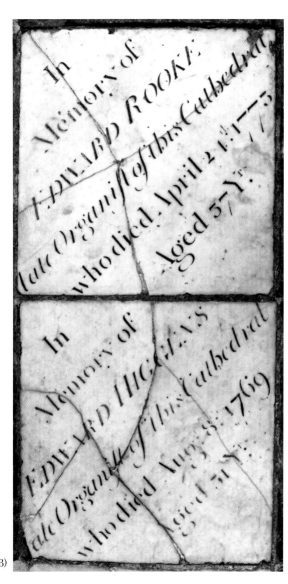

(DB)

Composers through the Ages

CHARLES WESLEY JNR AND SAMUEL WESLEY

Bristol is very proud to be able to claim Charles Wesley, the great hymnwriter, as one of its sons for many years. He moved to Bristol to be 'Minister in Residence' at the New Rooms in 1749. With Sarah, his young wife, he fathered many children, but the two children that concern us are Charles Wesley Junior and Samuel. Their early musical education mostly took place in the family home in Bristol. The boys' earliest musical influence was their mother, who had a good singing voice and played the harpsichord. Although Charles junior is much less well known than his brother, he was, like Samuel, regarded as a musical prodigy in childhood, and he was playing the organ before the age of three.

The first music teachers for these two prodigies were both local church organists. From around the age of six, Charles junior had lessons from Edward Rooke, who was Organist at All Saints' Church from 1759 and then later at Bristol Cathedral from 1769 to 1773. Charles junior's public performances in Bristol included an Easter 1774 organ concerto in Bristol Cathedral. On that occasion Samuel was notably aggrieved, as he had expected to be the one giving the performance. It wasn't the only time that Samuel's nose was put out of joint. Below is an amusing poem written by the eight-year-old boy when, because of his tender years, he was withdrawn from a performance of an oratorio performed before the Corporation in Bristol. It's not surprising that Samuel turns to verse in extremis: his grandfather was a poet and his father had written 6,500 hymns. I suppose it would probably be fair to describe

Samuel as a 'handful'! In 1784 he became a Roman Catholic 'for musical rather than doctrinal reasons', which unsurprisingly resulted in estrangement from his father Charles until the latter's death in 1788.

An Epistle to my much respected friend, Dr Ludlow, by S. Wesley

To you, dear Doctor, I appeal,
To all the tuneful city,
Am I not used extremely ill
By Musical Committee?

Why it's enough to make one wild:
They court and then refuse me,
They advertise and call me child,
And as a child they use me.

Excusing their contempt, they say,
Which more inflames my passion,
I am not grave enough to play
Before the Corporation.

To their sweet city waits, altho'
I may not hold a candle,
I question if their worships know
The odds 'twixt me and Handel.

A child of eight years old, I grant
I am but light and giddy,
The solidness of Burgrum want
The steadiness of Liddy.

Detail from window in south aisle of nave. (DB)

SAMUEL WESLEY
ORGANIST AND COMPOSER
BORN IN BRISTOL 1766

Yet quick perhaps as other folks
I can assign a reason
And keep my time as well as Stokes
And come as much in season.

With Bristol organists – not yet
I stand in competition,
Like them, you know, I would be great
And do not want ambition.

Spirit I do not want, nor will
Upon a just occasion,
To make the rash despisers feel
My weight of indignation.

The trodden worm will turn again
And shall I not resent it?
Who gave the sore affront in vain
They would with tears repent it.

Nothing shall e'er appease my rage
At their unjust demeanour,
Unless they prudently assuage
My anger with a Steiner.

Musical Times vol. 48, no. 768, 1907, p.91

WESLEY IN F

Samuel Wesley became the most celebrated organist of his day, and those who heard this diminutive but dignified man play would say that there were many good organists, but none was able to move the listener as 'Old Sam' could.

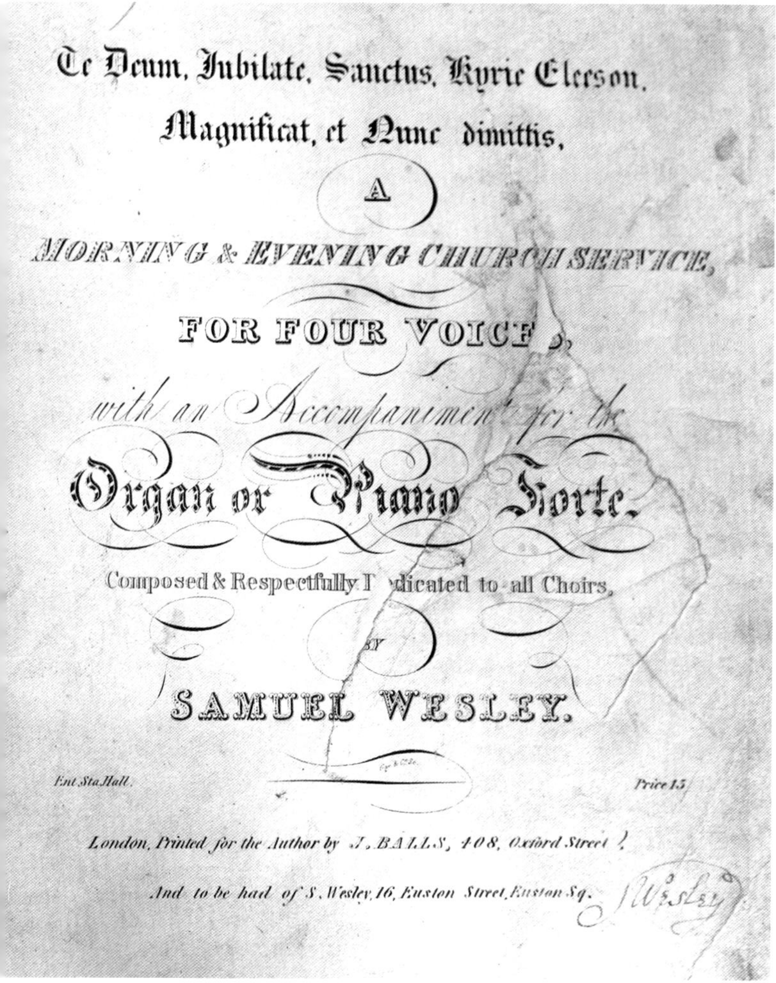

Te Deum, Jubilate, Sanctus, Kyrie Eleeson,

Magnificat, et Nunc dimittis,

A

MORNING & EVENING CHURCH SERVICE,

FOR FOUR VOICES,

with an Accompaniment for the

Organ or Piano Forte.

Composed & Respectfully Dedicated to all Choirs,

BY

SAMUEL WESLEY.

Ent. Sta. Hall.

Price 15

London, Printed for the Author by J. BALLS, 408, Oxford Street

And to be had of S. Wesley, 16, Euston Street, Euston Sq.

A signed copy of Samuel Wesley's Morning and Evening Service

He converted to Roman Catholicism in 1784, hence much of his sacred music was written for that Church. Fortunately, ecumenism has always existed in music and his compositions have been and are still performed in Anglican cathedrals such as Bristol, especially the two Latin anthems, 'In exitu Israel' and 'Exultate Deo'. Indeed, Samuel Wesley, being a professional musician, was anxious to write music to be performed, no matter where.

In the library at Bristol Cathedral there is a copy of his Service in F, bound in hard boards, with 'Lay Clerk Dec' written in pencil at the top of the title page. At the foot of that page is Wesley's signature, but it is difficult to tell whether this is printed or specifically written. One would like to think that it is his authentic signature and that he gave this as a gift to one of his friends at the Cathedral in Bristol.

The Service in F, published in 1824 when Wesley was in London, consists, as the title page tells us, of a 'Te Deum, Jubilate, Sanctus, Kyrie Eleison, Magnificat, et Nunc dimittis', and is 'Composed & Respectfully Dedicated to all Choirs'. The style is typical of what was accepted for music in the Church at the time, though Wesley was criticised for returning to the style of Purcell and Blow and for daring to use such things as false relations (a 'chromatic contradiction' between two notes sounding simultaneously, or in close proximity, in two different voices or parts). There are numerous felicities in this service: for example there is the rather abrupt change of keys (especially the use of C minor) in the Sanctus, the pause between 'For behold from henceforth' and 'All Generations shall call me blessed' in the Magnificat, and the eight bars of melismas on the word 'Glory' in the Nunc Dimittis. Certainly it is a setting at least some of which should be in the repertoire in his home city.

WILLIAM BOYCE'S 'CATHEDRAL MUSIC'

Cathedral Music
Being a collection in score of the
Most Valuable and Useful Compositions
For that Service, by the
Several English Masters
of the last Two Hundred Years.
The Whole Selected and Carefully Revis'd
By Dr. William Boyce,
Organist and Composer to the Royal Chapels, and
Master of his Majesty's Band of Musicians.
(Preface to Volume I)

Towards the end of the eighteenth century, Cathedral musicians throughout the country were greatly assisted in their work by the advent of the mass printing of musical scores. William Boyce, sometime Master of the King's Music, published the final volume of his great collection *Cathedral Music* in 1773, and its influence was immense. Before its publication, musical scores had been transmitted in manuscript copies, which inevitably allowed for a great variety of interpretation. After Boyce's final volume, uniform texts could be obtained in print, and the beginnings of modern scholarship were firmly established.

The scope of Boyce's work was compendious, including biographies of the composers and scores for some 900 pieces dating from Henry VIII to Purcell and Child. Bristol's own Elway Bevin was represented by six works, including his Service in D Minor, which appeared alongside music by Tallis and Morley in Volume One. To this day, it remains one of the most ambitious surveys of English Church music ever undertaken. Boyce's own preface to the last volume describes the great changes that had occurred over the centuries, and may be paraphrased thus:

> [There was] a gravity in Church Music, having been particularly ordered in the reign of Queen Elizabeth … but on the return of King Charles the Second from his long exile in Foreign Countries, a lighter kind of Church Music prevailed, better suited to the gay disposition of that Monarch and his Court

The work was financed by subscription, and the Dean and Chapter of Bristol obtained their own copies. The first two volumes were supplied by Boyce himself on 24 February 1792.

SIR WALFORD DAVIES (MASTER OF THE KING'S MUSIC)

Although Walford Davies's tombstone in Bristol Cathedral's beautiful garden and churchyard may have sometimes been forgotten by others now that 70 years have passed since his death, nevertheless he still has something to say about music in general and cathedrals in particular. Walford Davies might reasonably have expected burial at Windsor or the Temple Church in London. However, the Second World War intervened, and suspended normal expectations of life or death or burial. So things were rather different for him.

Walford Davies was an outstanding all-rounder. He was knighted in 1922 and, following the death of Sir Edward Elgar in 1934, he was appointed Master of the King's Music. He was a

Sir Walford Davies's gravestone in the Cathedral garden. (DB)

composer of songs, church music, cantatas and orchestral music; he was a choirmaster at St George's, Windsor and the Temple, London (though never actually Organist at Bristol Cathedral); he was a festival adjudicator, a musicologist, an organist and a university Professor at Aberystwyth; he was also a broadcaster, and it is in this role that we start to feel ownership of him. He moved to Bristol with the BBC during the War – and one of the Lady Chapels became his studio and the Berkeley Chapel became his workshop.

He was more than competent in so many different areas. Strangely enough, being an all-rounder is something that cathedral buildings must always be. Cathedrals have to be places of prayer, theatres of grand worship and arenas for quiet meditation; they have to be concert halls, commercial centres and, in Bristol's case, quite often a graduation hall.

Not only was he an all-rounder, but Walford Davies had the gift of bringing together popular culture and high art, and the two are not easy bedfellows. From 1924 until his death he gave 428 of his famous music lessons through the new medium of broadcasting. He realised its hugely popular potential – 'He always seemed to come right into the room with us', said one listener. In an obituary, Sir Adrian Boult wrote:

Millions of listeners, young and old, have been encouraged by Sir Walford to listen to the best music. His uncanny gift of illuminating the great masterpieces in homely, non-technical language was the secret of his popularity.

HERBERT HOWELLS ('HILLS OF THE NORTH, REJOICE!')

The composer Herbert Howells has strong associations with the West of England. Born in Lydney in 1892, he studied initially with Sir Herbert Brewer at Gloucester Cathedral. After further study with Stanford, Parry and Charles Wood, he enjoyed a long life, gaining considerable international recognition, occasionally coloured by personal tragedy. A professional colleague of Elgar, and Vaughan Williams, Howells regarded his greatest achievement as his 'Hymnus Paradisi', written in memory of his son Michael, who died in 1935. Always associated with transcendent music for the Anglican Church, Howells was commissioned to compose a motet 'Take Him Earth for Cherishing' for the memorial service of President Kennedy in 1964.

'Hills of the North, Rejoice!' was commissioned by Clifton High School in 1977 and first performed by their choir on the occasion of the school's centenary service in the Cathedral. In fact, the genesis of the work dates from an earlier period when Howells first served at St Paul's Girls School, where he followed Gustav Holst as Director of Music. The words of Charles Oakley's famous advent hymn are expanded into a three-part setting with keyboard accompaniment, which Barry Rose has described as a 'virtuoso tour-de-force for upper-voice choirs'.

Written when Howells was in his 85th year, 'Hills of the North,

Herbert Howells
(1892-1983)

Hills of the North

Anthem for soprano (or treble) voices & organ

Commission for Clifton High School

Rejoice!' forms a companion piece to the equally late piece for organ called 'St Louis Comes to Clifton', which dates from the same year. The composer attended the première performance in the Cathedral, and later wrote that the 68-voice choir 'sang as if they loved it'. The music remains a Cathedral copyright to this day.

MALCOLM ARCHER ('AT THE ROUND EARTH'S IMAGINED CORNERS')

It was entirely fitting that Malcolm Archer was commissioned by the School Governors to compose a choral work to mark the opening of Bristol Cathedral Choir School. 'At the Round Earth's Imagined Corners' was written by that great seventeenth-century metaphysical poet and Dean of St Paul's, John Donne. He was noted for paradoxes, ironies and dramatic speech rhythms and for the celebration of life and its pleasures: 'Blow your trumpets, angels, and arise, arise from death you numberless infinities of souls.'

At the round earth's imagined corners

John Donne (1572-1631)

Malcolm Archer (b.1952)

The setting of 'At the Round Earth's Imagined Corners', proved to be a wonderful celebratory musical composition that provided the perfect musical backcloth to the formal opening of Bristol Cathedral Choir School in the presence of the Princess Royal on 22 February 2010.

Malcolm Archer was Organist and Master of Choristers of Bristol Cathedral Choir during the 1980s before going on to Wells Cathedral and then St Paul's Cathedral. He followed on from Hubert Hunt and Clifford Harker as part of a continuum of outstanding composers to have led music at Bristol Cathedral.

PHILIP WILBY

Philip Wilby has been closely associated with the music in Bristol Cathedral since his wife Wendy became Precentor in 2007. At Oxford he was encouraged to compose by Herbert Howells and soon after leaving was invited to join the music staff of Leeds University by the Professor, Alexander Goehr. Philip was eventually made a Professor of Composition there in 2002. In the words of the Black Dyke Band, with whom he has worked for 22 years, Philip is 'the master musician'. A professional string player at one stage, an acting cathedral organist at another, his Honorary Fellowship of the Royal School of Church Music shows just how many of Philip's choral works are expressions of a strongly held Christian faith. They range from the recently commissioned oratorio on St John the Baptist (libretto by the Bristol Canon Emeritus, Neville Boundy) or the 'Brontë Mass', recorded by David Hill and the Bach Choir, to the simplicity of the anthem 'Make me a light', written for the Junior Choir of Thorner Parish Church in Yorkshire and now a popular item with the Cathedral's outreach choir 'Bristol Voices'.

During his time in Bristol, he has composed several pieces for the Cathedral musicians, including a setting of George Herbert's 'Prayer' for men's voices, which was included in the Bristol Choir

Philip Wilby

Book, and a set of responses. Several of his pieces have found their way into the current repertoire. His setting of 'The Earth is the Lord's' heralded the Wilbys' arrival at Wendy's installation service in Bristol Cathedral, and this composition was eventually broadcast by the Cathedral Choir as part of BBC Radio 3's 'Choral Evensong'.

DAVID BEDNALL

Because of the enduring nature of their art, composers have left an indelible mark on the music and worship of Bristol Cathedral. Historically, this has been true for many generations, and it is significant that their work is still valued to the present day. The current Sub-Organist at Bristol is David Bednall, whose celebrated compositional activities have taken the Cathedral's reputation far and wide and whose music is often heard in our services.

David Bednall

Educated at Sherborne School and Queens College Oxford, he worked at Gloucester and Wells cathedrals before taking up his present role as Sub-Organist in Bristol in tandem with doctoral studies at the University. His compositions have been widely distributed on CD, and Matthew Owens and the choir of Wells Cathedral have recorded a critically acclaimed CD of his choral music for Regent Records called *Hail, Gladdening Light*. This recording was awarded the accolade 'Editor's Choice' in *Gramophone* magazine, and has led to a number of subsequent projects, including first recordings of Bednall's 'Requiem', his ambitious Christmas composition 'Welcome All Wonders' and a further collaboration with Wells entitled 'Flame Celestial'.

The musical style of Bednall's compositions draws on several well-digested and attractive influences, combining English heritage with more Francophile treatments of plainsong. His sound world has been described as showing 'considerable variety, from dense and evocative mysticism, to innocent exuberance, and to timeless serenity'.

For the retirement of Dean Robert Grimley in 2009, Bednall contributed an anthem to the Bristol Choir book, embracing the original values of the Augustinian foundation and called 'I am the Light of the World'. This was subsequently broadcast by the Cathedral Choir on BBC Radio 3's 'Choral Evensong'.

Musicians and Hymnwriters

SAMUEL CROSSMAN (HYMNWRITER)

Samuel Crossman was briefly Dean of Bristol Cathedral between 1682 and 1684 and he is buried in the South Aisle. According to the records, his daughter Elizabeth, who died at the age of thirteen, also has a tombstone in the Cathedral, on which is the inscription, in Latin: 'The Hope and Delight of her parents – gone on before, we follow.'

Nicholas 1639 · Henry Glemham 1660 Richard Towgood 1667 · Samuel Crossman 1683 · Richard Thomson 1684 · William Levett 1686 · George Royse 1694

Detail from window in the Chapter House

Crossman was born at Bradfield Monachorum in Suffolk in 1623 or 1624 and it was in Suffolk that he spent most of his life after leaving Pembroke College, Cambridge. He was Rector of All Saints Church in Sudbury in 1647, but being a leading Puritan he was ejected when the Act of Uniformity was passed in 1662. However – and one cannot help being reminded of the Vicar of Bray when one reads about him, as he always seems to have had a foot in both camps – he was reordained by the Bishop of Norwich in 1665, and was given the curacy of St Gregory's and St Peter's in Sudbury, as well as being made one of the King's chaplains. In 1667 he became a Prebendary of Bristol Cathedral, later becoming its Treasurer and then Dean.

The reason Crossman qualifies for being included in a musical history of Bristol Cathedral is that amongst his writings are a number of hymns, and one in particular is regularly performed in the Cathedral – 'My song is love unknown'. This hymn seems always to have been popular, though only since 1918 has it been sung to John Ireland's magnificent tune, which the composer himself called 'Love unknown'.

WILLIAM CHATTERTON DIX (HYMNWRITER)

William Chatterton Dix was born in Bristol, England on 14 June 1837, the son of a surgeon. His father had written a biography of the poet Thomas Chatterton, who lived in Bristol, and he gave his son the poet's surname as a middle name in his honour. Young William attended Bristol Grammar School, and after he left school he became the manager of a marine insurance company in Glasgow, a vocation which he followed to the end of his life.

However, his heart was in hymnwriting and he wrote more than 40 hymns over the course of his life. It has been said of him: 'Few modern writers have shown so signal a gift as his for the difficult art of hymn-writing.' Dix also wrote many Christmas and Easter carols, the most widely known of which is 'As with gladness men of old'. Another Dix hymn sung regularly by the choir and congregation of the Cathedral is 'Hallelujah, sing to Jesus'. Both of these hymns are mentioned on his wall memorial, which is to be found at the west end of the Cathedral. He died on 9 September, 1898 in Cheddar, Somerset, and was buried in Cheddar Parish Church.

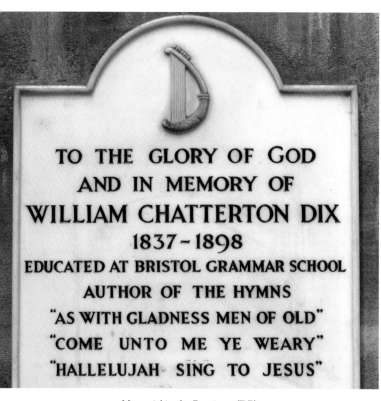

TO THE GLORY OF GOD
AND IN MEMORY OF
WILLIAM CHATTERTON DIX
1837~1898
EDUCATED AT BRISTOL GRAMMAR SCHOOL
AUTHOR OF THE HYMNS
"AS WITH GLADNESS MEN OF OLD"
"COME UNTO ME YE WEARY"
"HALLELUJAH SING TO JESUS"

Memorial in the Baptistry. (DB)

CATHERINE WINKWORTH (HYMNWRITER)

Memorial Tablet in Bristol Cathedral:

In Memory of
CATHERINE WINKWORTH
Who, in her Lyra Germanica,
Rendering into English verse
The treasures of German sacred poetry,
Opened a new source of light, consolation, and strength
In many thousand homes.
Her works reveal a clear and harmonious intellect
A gift of true poetic insight and expression,
And the firm Christian faith
Which was the mainspring of a life
Rich in tender and affectionate ministration
And fruitful in various fields of active service.
Her loss is mourned by all who shared her labours,
And by the many friends whom death has bereft
Of her rare sympathy, her wise counsel,
Her bright companionship, and her unfailing help
In every time of need.
To commemorate her work, and to perpetuate
Her efforts for the better education of women,
A scholarship, bearing her name,
Has been founded in University College, Bristol
By friends who now dedicate this table
To her memory
Born in London, September 13th, 1827
Died in Monnetier, Savoy, July lst, 1878
'The child has now its Father seen,
And feels what kindling love may be,
And knoweth what those words may mean,
"Himself, the Father, loveth thee".

IN MEMORY OF

CATHERINE WINKWORTH

WHO IN HER LYRA GERMANICA
RENDERING INTO ENGLISH VERSE
THE TREASURES OF GERMAN SACRED POETRY,
OPENED A NEW SOURCE OF LIGHT, CONSOLATION AND STRENGTH
IN MANY THOUSAND HOMES.

HER WORKS REVEAL A CLEAR AND HARMONIOUS INTELLECT
A GIFT OF TRUE POETIC INSIGHT AND EXPRESSION
AND THE FIRM CHRISTIAN FAITH
WHICH WAS THE MAINSPRING OF A LIFE
RICH IN TENDER AND AFFECTIONATE MINISTRATION
AND FRUITFUL IN VARIOUS FIELDS OF ACTIVE SERVICE.

HER LOSS IS MOURNED BY ALL WHO SHARED HER LABOURS
AND BY THE MANY FRIENDS WHOM DEATH HAS BEREFT
OF HER RARE SYMPATHY, HER WISE COUNSEL,
HER BRIGHT COMPANIONSHIP AND HER UNFAILING HELP
IN EVERY TIME OF NEED.

TO COMMEMORATE HER WORK, AND TO PERPETUATE
HER EFFORTS FOR THE BETTER EDUCATION OF WOMEN
A SCHOLARSHIP BEARING HER NAME
HAS BEEN FOUNDED IN UNIVERSITY COLLEGE BRISTOL
BY FRIENDS WHO NOW DEDICATE THIS TABLET
TO HER MEMORY.

BORN IN LONDON SEPTEMBER 13TH 1827
DIED AT MONNETIER IN SAVOY JULY 1ST 1878.

"THE CHILD HATH NOW ITS FATHER SEEN,
AND FEELS WHAT KINDLING LOVE MAY BE
AND KNOWETH WHAT THOSE WORDS MAY MEAN;
'HIMSELF, THE FATHER, LOVETH THEE'"

LYRA GERMANICA

TYLEY, OF BRISTOL

This memorial tablet needs a little unpacking. It can be found at the east end of the North Choir Aisle on the wall there. This talented lady lived for much of her life in Manchester with her family, but, with the breakdown of her father's health, she eventually came with the family to Clifton, where she was deeply involved in promoting women's rights. She was the Secretary of the Clifton Association for Higher Education for Women and a supporter of the Clifton High School for Girls, where a house is named after her. She was likewise Governor of the Red Maids' School in Westbury-on-Trym, whose pupils still attend the Cathedral regularly.

We know of Catherine Winkworth through numerous translations of German hymns included in her 1855 publication *Lyra Germanica*. A further collection followed in 1858. *The New English Hymnal* contains six of her translations, including Joachim Neander's 'Praise to the Lord, the Almighty, the King of creation' and Martin Rinkart's 'Now thank we all our God', both regularly sung in Bristol Cathedral.

As a hymnwriter she is commemorated with John Mason Neale on the liturgical calendar of the Episcopal Church (USA) on 7 August and on the Calendar of Saints of the Evangelical Lutheran Church in America on 1 July. Sadly the Church of England's Common Worship Calendar does not include her name. According to *The Harvard University Hymn Book*, Winkworth 'did more than any other single individual to make the rich heritage of German hymnody available to the English-speaking world'.

JOHN RAPHAEL PEACEY

John Raphael Peacey ended his interesting career by being appointed Residentiary Canon of Bristol Cathedral after the Second World War in 1945. Born in 1896 in Hove in Sussex, he fought in the First World War and was awarded the Military Cross. He became a scholar of Selwyn College, Cambridge, gaining a First in Theology, and was ordained as a priest in 1923.

Born in Sussex, he was a good enough cricketer to make four appearances for the county side between 1920 and 1922, though his overall batting average of nine in those games does not perhaps enhance his reputation! After his ordination he worked briefly in the Diocese of Oxford, at the same time holding the position of an Assistant Master at Wellington College. Then followed a successful academic career at Selwyn College, between 1923 and 1927, where he became Fellow, Dean and Precentor. In 1927 he went out to India as Head Master of the Bishop Cotton School at Simla, and in 1934 he became Principal of the Bishop's College in Calcutta.

Returning to England at the end of World War II he was appointed to Bristol Cathedral, where he was a Residentiary Canon between 1945 and 1966. Between his retirement in 1967 and his death in 1971 he took to writing hymns, several of which are in use today, especially 'Awake, awake, fling off the night', which is based on *Ephesians* 5, and 'Go forth for God, go to the world in peace', very suitable for an ordination, and 'For Mary, mother of our Lord'.

Go forth for God, go to the world in peace;
Be of good courage, armed with heavenly grace,
In God's good Spirit daily to increase,
Till in his kingdom we behold his face.
Sing praise to him who brought us on our way,
Sing praise to him who bought us with his blood,
Sing praise to him who sanctifies each day,
Sing praise to him who reigns one Lord and God.

DR EDWARD HODGES (ORGANIST)

The image you see here shows part of Bristol Cathedral Choir School and is known as the Pates building. It occupies the southern side of Cloister Garth. In 1824 Dr Edward Hodges moved into it, being as it was the Prebendal House belonging to Lord William Somerset, Canon of the Cathedral.

Dr Hodges was a fine Bristol musician who had previously occupied Prior's Lodge by the Abbey Gateway, but it seems that his professional story was clouded by constant disappointment. A polymath who could turn his hand to so much, he wasn't employed by the Cathedral but made a living primarily as an organist and composer in Bristol churches, yet longing all the time for greater things – for St George's, Windsor, for Exeter Cathedral … but sadly these positions never came his way. This eventually led to him crossing the Atlantic to the Americas, ultimately ending up as Organist at Trinity Church, Wall Street, New York. This, of course, was the church that was to become so significant in 9/11 because of its proximity to Ground Zero.

Dr Hodges was undoubtedly inspired and stimulated by the ancient Cathedral cloisters where he lived in the 1820s and '30s. His daughter, Faustina, leaves us with a fascinating biography of her father. With a characteristically creative and poetic style, she writes with deep affection and admiration about her father. She particularly speaks of him walking in the cloisters in the moonlight: 'There was something fascinating to him in all this, and here he used to walk and meditate at night, when no sound broke the stillness but the watchman's rather plaintive cry, and the regular sound of the Cathedral quarter-bell.' She continually quotes from his diary, which reveals not only a profound Christian faith but also a touching vulnerability. The entries offer a first-class picture of Bristol life and some of its visiting musicians. The first day of October 1829 provoked this entry:

I proceeded with my brother Archelaus to Redcliff Church, where we witnessed the really astounding performance of Samuel Wesley upon the noble organ therein. It was the most wonderful I ever heard, more even than I had before been capable of conceiving; the flow of melody, the stream of harmony, was so complete, so unbroken, so easy, and yet so highly wrought and so superbly scientific, that I was altogether knocked off my stilts. Before such a man and organist I am less than nothing and vanity. No words can sound his praises too highly. He is the Prince of Musicians and Emperor of Organists.

41

CLARA BUTT (CONTRALTO)

Dame Clara Butt was the most distinguished contralto of her generation. Born in 1872 and educated at South Bristol High School, she won a scholarship to the Royal College of Music in 1890. Whilst she was in London, Queen Victoria heard her sing and subsequently financed three months further study for her in Paris. On the concert stage, she enjoyed enormous success, and Elgar composed his 'Sea Pictures' for her in 1899.

In addition to art songs, Clara Butt also included popular items in her programmes, and her career coincided with growing public enthusiasm for the gramophone. Her recordings of Sullivan's 'Lost Chord' and 'Abide with me' became instant successes. Later, in the patriotic fervour surrounding the Great War, her recordings of 'Land of Hope and Glory' and 'Rule Brittania' became legendary. Her Bristol connections are commemorated by a blue plaque at the family home at 3 Belle Vue, Totterdown.

Famously, Dame Clara enjoyed the distinction of being the first to be married in Bristol Cathedral's newly opened nave in 1900. The Cathedral Marriage Registers show both her name and that of her husband, the baritone Kennerly Rumford. Clara turned down the opportunity to be married in St Paul's Cathedral in favour of her childhood home, and many local factories and shops closed to allow their staff to attend the ceremony. Queen Victoria sent a wedding gift, and Sir Arthur Sullivan composed music for the ceremony. The City of Bristol gave Dame Clara a diamond brooch ingeniously linking her initials, CB, with the City of Bristol.

In recognition of her wartime work in aid of the Red Cross and other service charities, Clara Butt was appointed Dame Commander of the Order of the British Empire in 1920. She died in 1936.

Clara Butt preparing for a performance

42

'DAN' ROOTHAM (LAY CLERK)

One expects, in writing about the history of a cathedral's music, to be discussing organists, composers and possibly scholars (such as E.H. Fellowes in the case of Bristol; see entry no. 66). It should not, however, be forgotten that originally the organist did not have the exalted position he or she has now, and often it was one of the choir men, be they called Lay Clerks, Songmen or Vicars Choral, who played the organ when necessary. This meant that the training of the boys was then in the hands of a singer rather than an organist.

As far as Bristol Cathedral is concerned there was one outstanding Lay Clerk, who contributed hugely to music not only in the Cathedral but also in the city, and that was Daniel Wilberforce Rootham, always known as 'Dan'. He was born in Cambridge in 1837 (coincidentally the year of the founding of the Bristol Madrigal Society – see entry no. 56), where his father was a bass in the choirs of both Trinity and St John's Colleges. At Cambridge he sang as a treble in both those choirs and received his musical tuition from Thomas Attwood Walmisley of 'D Minor' fame. On his father's death in 1852 he moved to Bristol, where his older brother, Samuel, was a tenor Lay Clerk and Dan soon was appointed as a bass Lay Clerk, in which position he remained until 1877.

In 1865 he succeeded J.D. Corfe, the Cathedral organist, as conductor of the Bristol Madrigal Society, in spite of the request of S.S. Wesley to be considered for the post, and he remained conductor until his retirement in 1915. Rootham had been helping Corfe look after the boys in the Cathedral Choir, which is probably why he was preferred to Wesley. He also held the post of organist at St Peter's, Clifton Wood, for 27 years from 1866. In the 1870s he played an important part in the setting up and conducting of the Bristol Festival Choir, some 300-400 strong.

Rootham taught singing in Bristol, and Clara Butt and Eva Turner were among his pupils. An accomplished linguist and elocutionist,

Cathedral burial register

he also taught 'Voice Management' at Wells Theological College. His daughter Mabel was the first Bristol Scholar at the Royal College of Music; his son, Cyril Bradley, a pupil of Bristol Grammar School and Clifton College, succeeded Walford Davies as organist of Christ Church, Hampstead, and then in 1901 became organist of St John's College, Cambridge, where Cyril remained until his death in 1938.

43

THE CITY TRUMPETERS

Bristol's City Trumpeters are regular welcome visitors to the Cathedral, and accompany the Lord Mayor and Mace Bearer for the annual Legal Service, as well as attending the annual Rush Sunday Service at St Mary Redcliffe. Their livery is designed for riding, complete with riding hat and jodhpurs.

The late Norman Golding, who served as City Trumpeter for 64 years, handed over his position to his son Norman in 2010. The young James Bolton-Jones joined Norman in 2012. In July 2007, when the world-famous Black Dyke Band gave two performances in the Cathedral, they were proud to welcome both City Trumpeters as their guests.

The trumpeters perform a traditional 'Bristol City Fanfare', which has been designed to be played on a historic valveless natural trumpet. A pair of original silver trumpets, pitched higher than is now normal, and dating from 1715, are preserved as part of the City Regalia. Made by John Harris in London, they are contemporaneous with the first ecclesiastical performance of Handel's 'Messiah' in the Cathedral in 1758. Further information on these historic instruments may be found in the *Galpin Society Journal* (1965). The Civic Trumpets used today are also 'fanfare-shaped' with long, straight tubes and may support a banner; in common with all modern instruments they use three conventional valves.

The City Trumpeters. Photograph by David Harries

44

THE BRISTOL ENSEMBLE

Currently, if there *was* an orchestra-in-residence at Bristol Cathedral, it would be the Bristol Ensemble (formerly known as the Emerald Ensemble). Formed in 1994 by the entrepreneurial violinist Roger Huckle, the Bristol Ensemble is a musicians' collective, bringing together the best of the region's performers. It is marketed on their website as Bristol's professional chamber orchestra, and the Cathedral certainly uses it as such. The group is a very familiar and welcome Cathedral visitor, accompanying annual performances of 'Messiah' at Christmas time over a number of years. These have proved to be so successful with Bristol audiences that two successive evenings are booked in well ahead.

The Ensemble also almost always features in the High Sheriff's Concert held each June in the Cathedral. With this prestigious concert on the horizon, which traditionally has a regular attendance of many of the 'movers and shakers' of the city, the Ensemble's active and innovative education programme springs into action. It gathers together numerous schoolchildren from round and about to prepare them to take part alongside international artists.

The Bristol Ensemble playing in the Cathedral

Choirs

EARLIEST KNOWN PHOTOGRAPH OF THE CATHEDRAL CHOIR, 1864

CHOIR OF BRISTOL CATHEDRAL,
With Choristers, Lay Clerks, &c.

LEFT.	CHORISTERS.		RIGHT.
Master J. S. Churchill	1 ..		Master F. J. Insall
„ W. H. Bolt	2 ..		„ W. H. Cowlin
„ A. Smith	3 ..		„ T. P. Hook
„ J. Holder	4 ..		„ R. M. Fox
„ W. F. Spratt	— ..	(absent)	„ H. F. Barrett
„ J. E. J. Pavey	5 ..		„ H. Spratt

LAY CLERKS.

Mr. Rootham	1 ..	Mr. Greenwood
„ D. W. Rootham	2 ..	„ G. Gay
„ Collins	3 ..	„ Merrick
„ Yates	4 ..	„ France

Minor Canon. Rev. F. C. Skey.

Published by H. FRANCE,
Bookseller, &c., 64, PARK STREET, BRISTOL.

By kind permission of
Bristol Record Office

46

MOST RECENT PHOTOGRAPH
OF THE CATHEDRAL CHOIR
2012

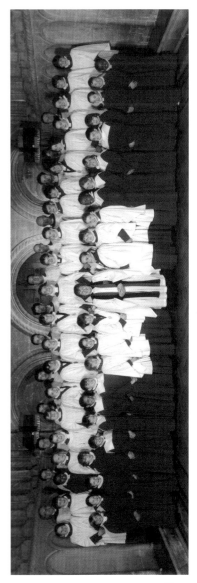

ESTABLISHING THE CATHEDRAL CHOIR AND THE CATHEDRAL STATUTES

From its foundation by Henry VIII in 1542, the importance of music in the Cathedral services was emphasized. The 38 Statutes which were to govern all aspects of Cathedral life were issued by the King in 1544. They stressed that every day the praise of God should be celebrated with song and rejoicing, and with hymns, Psalms and continual prayer. The King envisaged a community of Dean, Canons, Minor Canons, Lay Clerks and Boy Choristers, together with their servants, living a communal life very similar to that of the Augustinian Canons whose Abbey had transformed into the Cathedral.

To maintain the regular daily round of choral services, the Statutes ordered that there should be a Precentor to supervise the choir, 'that no discord may arise in the chanting'. As well as six Canons, there were to be six Minor Canons and six Lay Clerks. They were to be 'men skilled in singing, being approved as such by the judgement of those who, in the same church, do well understand the art of music'. The King ordered that the choir should also include 'six boys of tender age, with good and promising voices, who may serve, minister and sing'. For their instruction a Choirmaster was to be appointed 'of good life and reputation, skilful both in singing and playing upon the organ, who shall diligently spend his time in instructing the boys'. Finally, the educational provision of the newly established Cathedral was to be completed by the appointment of a Master and an Under-Master, 'skilful in Latin and Greek, of good fame and a goodly life, well qualified for teaching'. They were to provide an education for 'those boys who shall resort to our school to learn grammar'.

The King's detailed orders for the maintenance of a communal life did not survive the major religious changes of the short reign of Edward VI (1547-53). Nonetheless, the Statutes remained in force and are still observed more than four-and-a-half centuries later.

Window in the Cloister

BOY CHORISTERS

For many, the picture of 'the boy chorister' is an iconic one, suggesting romantic images of cathedrals, innocence, angels and candles. This gentle, cherubic picture belies the dedication, relentless hard work and iron discipline that has accompanied this favourite image ever since boys sang in honour of the Virgin Mary in Lady Chapels in pre-Reformation times.

St Augustine's Abbey undoubtedly had a few boy singers linked with the Eastern Lady Chapel. The surviving Compotus Rolls give us snippets of information about these singing boys. It seems that in the fifteenth century there were between three and six such boys, who were joined by a few adult Lay Clerks in order to sing the new polyphonic music. About this date, and for the first time, the place where the boys were being taught is referred to as The Grammar School, so in fact there would have been a Senior Canon teaching the novices, a Master of the Boys, probably a layman, and a Grammar Master teaching the young Canons, choristers and a handful of other boys.

The Monastery was dissolved in 1539 and the Cathedral established in 1542, with the Statutes being drawn up in 1544. The Grammar School was part of the scheme. There was to be one Master of the Choristers, six choristers and two Grammar Masters, one being the Headmaster and the other an usher or Under-master.

The Statutes go on to stipulate various payments: 6s per month was to be allowed for the board of the Headmaster and the Master of the Choristers and 4s 8d per month for the Under-master. For clothing, the Headmaster was allowed four yards of cloth for his gown and the Under-master three yards and to each chorister two yards. Stipends were allotted thus: The Headmaster was to receive £8 8s 8d per year, the Under-master 59s 2d and each of the choristers 15s. Thus begins the music budget! Music in Bristol Cathedral nowadays forms about a fifth of the annual Cathedral running costs, with the clothing of choristers forming a significant part of that.

Ralph Sansum, Head Boy Chorister

Jumping ahead to the nineteenth century, there was a chronic shortage of candidates for voice trials – so that, in 1840, prospective choristers had to be picked from those boys already in the school. By 1857 the Dean and Chapter paid the Headmaster six guineas for every chorister over the number of 10, but towards the end of the century the shortage was so great that the Governors discussed testing every new boy entering the school for singing ability.

School hours were fixed at 9 am to 10.45 am and 2 pm to 2.45 pm, between which the choristers fitted in Matins and Evensong and practice time. Eventually, there were 18 choristers educated free of charge, the others paid either £2 a term or £5 per year. By 1875, school numbers had sunk to just these 18 choristers and only a few other boys. However, with the appointment of Mr William Henry Pate as Headmaster, the tide began to turn. Numbers rose rapidly and in 1879 two Assistant Masters were appointed. By January of that year (at that time the school year began in January) it was decided to limit the intake to 100 boys. They were now taken at eight years old, and the choristers even earlier. A few boarders were taken and they were lodged in the Headmaster's house.

The daily routine for the choristers in the early twentieth century was harder than it is today. They worked a seven-day week and sang two services a day, except for Friday Evensong, which was said. Matins was at 9 am, followed by an hour's practice. Evensong followed the end of school at 4 pm and on Sundays there were three services. After this they had three hours 'home lessons'. In all they missed about 12 hours schooling every week. Nevertheless, all seemed to do well in later life. This extract from the *Musical Times* in November 1907 is enlightening:

> The choristers were always in the Cathedral for the first two hours of each day, under Mr George Riseley, organist and choirmaster. By this arrangement they missed the early Latin lessons. At that time the full choir sang the morning services every day, and in the afternoons as well, and this was continued for many years.

Now, in the twenty-first century, it is still a requirement for a chorister to be a student at Bristol Cathedral Choir School. However, the duties for the boys are much reduced because they are shared out in equal proportions with the girl choristers. That clear sound of choristers' voices echoing around the cloisters just before Matins continues, and it contributes hugely to the ambiance and sense of spiritual purpose in the building. In Bristol we recognise that this is a precious but vulnerable sound.

GIRL CHORISTERS

The 1990s saw an extraordinary revolution occurring in cathedrals where girls and women were concerned. The first-ever ordination service of women to the priesthood in England took place on 12 March 1994, and this momentous service very proudly took place in Bristol Cathedral, followed by many other such services around the country.

However, Bristol doesn't hold the accolade for introducing the first girl chorister. In 1991, the same year in which the 900th anniversary of the founding of the very first boys' choir in Britain was celebrated, Salisbury became the first English cathedral to form a separate and independent foundation for girl choristers. They sang their first service in October of that year. Things developed and nowadays the weekly services there are equally divided between the boy and girl choristers.

In Bristol, 1993 saw the birth of the Girls' Choir, consisting of girls aged from 10 to 18 years, which, with hard work and great enthusiasm, rapidly attained the necessary standard to sing in the Cathedral under the skilled direction of Robert Latham. These girls came on a voluntary basis from other secondary schools in Bristol; they faithfully rehearsed on Thursday evenings and sang occasional Evensongs, but they were not part of the Cathedral Choir as such. It took the Cathedral until September 2006 to introduce

Primrose Basvi. Girl Chorister

girl choristers into the Foundation, and that was when the Choir School became co-educational. It proved to be a rather slow beginning, but by 2010 the girl choristers were fully established, singing 50 per cent of the services and receiving the equivalent of the boy choristers in incentives.

The girls have been an easily justifiable addition to the life of the Cathedral and really are very much appreciated. It is wonderful that nowadays girls can be offered exactly the same opportunities as boys where the music of the Cathedral is concerned. The two top lines are not identical. The sound is different – there's no denying that – and the development and social interraction of each set of choristers is proving to be profoundly different as well. However, the end result is equally as pleasing but in different ways. Occasionally, the boy and girl choristers sing together, particularly at the major festivals. The combined sound of 32 choristers with an additional 16 probationers amongst them is extremely thrilling. It is a joy then to see worship led by girls and boys, women and men, all serving God and representing a congregation which, of course, is made up of girls and boys, women and men.

LAY CLERKS AND SINGING MEN PART 1

Our great cathedrals have a long and majestic history of sung music in the liturgy, which is unique and the envy of the world. Our cathedral choristers attract nationwide attention from time to time, and the quality and consistency of their achievement is marvelled at, in a world where modern educational principles and techniques change with alarming frequency!

Of no less importance is the history of our singing men. This story starts in Bristol with the tradition of sung liturgy established by the Augustinian Canons who first built and used our building. We have an insight into their musical diet through the survival of ancient missals, fully illuminated and provided with a musical text. As one might expect, the music being offered in worship at this

Lay clerks singing up the tower on Ascension Day

time was plainsong.

At the foundation of Bristol Cathedral in 1542, Henry VIII continued and developed the musical tradition by making stipends available for 'an Organist, Quoristers, and Singingmen' to provide music for the daily liturgy. Since the original stipend was made, countless others have succeeded the original six singing men – John More, Thomas Sexten, Nicholas Crepulgate, John Morgan, John Bedell and John Archade – in serving the glory of God with the gift of their voices in the Cathedral Church of the Holy and Undivided Trinity, Bristol.

Today, Bristol Cathedral still has provision for six Lay Clerks, being two altos, two tenors and two basses, one of each voice for the two sides of the choir, Decani and Cantoris. They sing on five out of seven days in the week, and their number is supplemented by the addition of younger Choral Scholars who are students at

Bristol University, generally one of each voice, who sing alongside them in a supporting and learning capacity. As well as underpinning the two choirs of trebles at Bristol, one of boys and one of girls, they also sing alone at 'Men's Voices' each week and at solemn times in the Cathedral, such as Holy Week, when a glimpse of the Cathedral's ancient monastic past can be glimpsed once again.

LAY CLERKS AND SINGING MEN PART 2

Looking at the Chapter minutes in the history of the Cathedral, the subject of the singing men emerges constantly, particularly where money and behaviour is concerned. Some of the entries in the late eighteenth century make for interesting reading:

31 May 1774
Abraham Hooper, one of the Singingmen, having several times been admonished for neglect of duty without effect, the Dean and Chapter order that on the next complaint made against him, the said Abraham Hooper to be turned out immediately from being any longer a Singingman of this church.

This provoked a more strategic response by the Chapter:

26 June 1775
On which day the Subdean and Chapter admonished the Singingmen of this church in general for neglect of duty and laid a mulct or punishment of 6d for every time they absent from the Divine Service of this church and orders that on the next complaint made against any or either of them they or he will be immediately turn'd out from being any longer a Singingman of this church.

It is fascinating that the same miscreant of 1774, Abraham Hooper, had remained in post another fifteen years before he was punished thus:

> 7 December 1789
> Ordered that as Abraham Hooper, one of the Singingmen of this Cathedral, did not attend the service of the choir this day, nor has attended it for the last two years and upwards, there will be imposed on him a mulct of a portion of his salary from Michaelmas last proportionate to the times of his non-attendance, to continue in the same proportion, till his regular attendance and behaviour shall recommend him to the approbation of the Chapter.

It seems, then, that the Chapter's 'bark was often worse than its bite'.

FROM GIRLS' CHOIR TO CATHEDRAL CONSORT

In what became a 'new wave' of girls' choirs across the country, in 1993, Bristol Cathedral became one of the first cathedrals to establish a Cathedral Girls' Choir alongside the (then all-male) Cathedral Choir. Unlike the Cathedral Choir, whose choristers all attended Bristol Cathedral School, the Girls' Choir drew its membership from across the city of Bristol. At its peak, it had 26 members. The founder-director was Robert Latham. Under his direction, the choir was invited to lead worship in Westminster Abbey in January 1999, and they also sang at the Royal Maundy Service for Her Majesty the Queen later the same year in Bristol Cathedral. Their trip to Bordeaux in 1998 was a huge success, as was their visit to Paris in February 2000, where they sang a series of concerts and a Mass in Notre-Dame. In May 2002, as part of Bristol Cathedral Festival, they sang with the internationally renowned soprano, Emma Kirkby, at which time she agreed to become Patron of the Choir.

Robert retired in 2002 and Paul Walton, the Assistant Organist, took over as the choir's Director. At this time, the Cathedral Consort was formed, combining elements of the Cathedral Choir and

Cathedral Consort and *below*, Cathedral Girls' Choir

the Girls' Choir. Originally it was made up of sixth-form boys from Bristol Cathedral School, the majority of whom had been choristers in Bristol Cathedral Choir, along with the sixth-form members of the Cathedral Girls' Choir. The intention was to give them more experience, which would stand them in good stead when looking at university choral scholarships, for example. The lower voices were assisted by some of the Lay Clerks or Choral Scholars from the Cathedral Choir. The Consort rehearsed and sang Evensong, usually once a month.

Meanwhile, the Girls' Choir continued to go from strength to strength. It toured Belgium and Ireland, undertook its first commission to celebrate its tenth anniversary and took part in Bristol University's performance of William Mathias's 'This Worldes Joie', singing the upper-voice semi-chorus. Their contribution attracted much praise, including from the composer's widow and daughter, who were present.

All the cathedral choirs have changed radically in recent years. As stated before in a previous entry, in 2006, the Cathedral Choir took account of the new co-educational status of the school by introducing a new top line of girl choristers alongside the existing boy choristers. To reflect this change, as well as to provide more rehearsal and performance opportunities for the Cathedral Consort, which only met once a month, the Consort expanded in September 2009 to combine with the existing Girls' Choir in order to form a larger mixed-voice choir. Currently it rehearses weekly and sings Evensong usually twice a month. It uses the Choral Scholars from the Cathedral Choir as part of its alto, tenor and bass sections. Just as the Girls' Choir was always open to membership from across the city, rather than the one school, so the whole Consort is, too, thus providing an opportunity for any gifted young person in Bristol.

As well as these regular services, the opportunity to sing large-scale works with a big choir and orchestra is becoming part of the regular programme. The Girls' Choir had already joined with Bristol Cathedral Concert Choir (March 2009) and Bristol Cathedral Chamber Choir (December 2009) for performances of Monteverdi's 'Vespers' and Handel's 'Messiah'. There is now a regular link between the Consort and the Cathedral Concert Choir, which began in March 2010 with a performance of Brahms's Requiem. Subsequent performances have included Handel's 'Coronation Anthems', Verdi's Requiem, Bach's Mass in B Minor and Sir William Walton's 'Belshazzar's Feast'. The Consort undertook its first tour in February 2013, to Toulouse, which was highly successful.

FROM SPECIAL CHOIR TO BRISTOL CATHEDRAL CONCERT CHOIR

In common with many cathedrals, Bristol has had its own choral society for some 60 years. Bristol Cathedral Special Choir was formed in 1953 by Cathedral Organist, Clifford Harker, growing out of the Festival of Britain Chorus and the Phoenix Choir. It has changed over the years, as the role of Cathedral Organist has changed within the city, from a vast Huddersfield Choral Society type of choir to a smaller, auditioned group.

When Clifford Harker founded Bristol Cathedral Special Choir, his intention was to differentiate the choir from the Cathedral Choir, but to stress the relationship with the Cathedral. Harker's choir has always had as its conductor the Master of the Choristers and Organist of the Cathedral and, as its accompanist, his Assistant, but, of recent years, the meaning of 'special' has become obscure, even contentious, and it was felt the time had come to change the name.

The change was agreed at an Extraordinary General Meeting held at the Cathedral on Monday, 15 May 2006. There had already been preliminary meetings to agree on the principal of a name change and at the meeting members were asked to choose between Bristol Cathedral Chorus and Bristol Cathedral Concert Choir. The latter won the vote convincingly and it was agreed that it would be introduced from the beginning of the 2006/7 season. Bristol Cathedral Concert Choir sings from the standard chorale repertoire and most of the choir's concerts are given in the Cathedral.

For Bristol Cathedral, the twenty-first century has brought with it a greater awareness of its responsibilities where 'outreach' is concerned. Gone are the days when Deans and Residentiary Canons spent their time reading, researching and writing in their comfortable studies and then wandered over to the Cathedral for Choral Evensong, which was so nicely sung by a sort of 'personal' choir. Nowadays, Chapters are realistic about their tasks of Christian proclamation and welcome. They recognise the importance of reaching out into the community and learning from it as well as sharing with it some of the Cathedral's resources. 'Bristol Voices' is one such project, coming under the umbrella of the Cathedral's Music Department.

In the early years of this new millennium, collaboration took place between the Cathedral and the Cathedral School, UWE and the City Council involving a certain amount of sponsorship from Youth Music and Western Power. Musical projects were developed, and exciting community performances involving children took place. All was poised and the ground was prepared for the government's musical, educational and financial input – called 'Sing-up!'. Bristol was one of the first to receive a substantial grant to begin a more structured Chorister Outreach Programme and for a few years this programme flourished and was funded by government money.

Inevitably, after three years of 'plenty', there have been many more years of relying on our own resources. The Friends of the Cathedral stepped in with a grant that has gone a long way towards supporting this continuing outreach work. We have been proud to maintain the Monday junior outreach choir, which meets in the Cathedral School under the direction of Jane England, as well as the chorister visits to primary schools in the region – three schools per term. Laurie Stewart has overseen that work, coaching the children and staff as they prepare to visit the Cathedral for

Bristol Voices

informal concerts. There has been no doubt that Bristol Voices has helped children discover the sheer joy of singing together.

55

VISITING CHOIRS

There are times when the Cathedral Choir is on holiday, and Bristol often plays host to visiting choirs from far and wide. Of course, the city is very attractive to visitors, with its numerous leisure activities and historic points of maritime interest. Best of all, many of these are accessible on foot. The Royal School of Church Music provides a valued network on an international scale, and many of our summer visitors come from abroad. In 2012, for example, worshippers enjoyed a number of full-week residencies by choirs from America and Portugal, as well as visits from other cathedral consorts and numerous RSCM groups.

Touring with a choir can be an expensive undertaking, especially if the group comes from Australia or the US, and the whole process, including logistical planning and fund-raising, can take several years. Little wonder, then, that the full experience of fund-raising, travelling and singing binds every choir together in a special way. Equally, preparing a full week's music without major repetitions can also be a rare undertaking and extends the essential repertoire of all touring groups. Memorably, many of our singers from abroad have chosen to perform musical items from their home, and our visitors have often provided us with rare musical treats. Negro spirituals have rubbed shoulders with new settings of the Evening Canticles and enliven the music of the summer months. Organists are always thrilled to be allowed access to the full resources of our instrument and often bring a few cherished masterpieces with them.

Our visitors are always welcome guests and always appear keen to return. In spite of the growing economic pressure, the 'visiting choirs' diary remains fully booked for several years to come.

A visiting choir, complete with parish priest and verger, from the Church of the Holy Spirit, Marleyville, Pennsylvania, USA

56

BRISTOL MADRIGAL SOCIETY

The Bristol Madrigal Society must have its place in any history of the music in Bristol Cathedral. For the first 118 years of its existence it was conducted by Cathedral musicians: J.D. Corfe, 1837-65; Dan Rootham, 1865-1915; Hubert Hunt, 1915-45; Alwyn Surplice, 1946-9; and Clifford Harker, 1949-55. It had been formed to resurrect the music of the period of the great English madrigal composers, which at the time was hardly known. The term 'madrigals' could include, as it did in the time of Queen Elizabeth I, sacred music (the first singing meeting of the Society included Gibbons's 'Hosanna to the Son of David' as well as madrigals by Weelkes, Wilbye, Morley and others). In 1885, under Dan Rootham, the Society sang in the Albert Hall; Bernard Shaw wrote that its singers were

> admirably trained, and in good practice, their most difficult selections being sung with precision and without the least apparent anxiety or effort. The boys' voices are especially beautiful and even.

The boys, like many of the altos, tenors and basses, were drawn from various cathedral choirs, but from the Bristol choir in particular.

The autobiography of E.H. Fellowes, Precentor of Bristol Cathedral between 1897 and 1900 (see entry no. 66), makes it clear that his association with the BMS turned his musical tastes in a new direction, realising that such groups had access to only a fraction of the music of the Elizabethan period. He said: 'It was at these meetings that I first perceived how the rhythmic and other characteristic features of Tudor music were misunderstood.' The result was his 36 volumes of *The English Madrigal School*.

The Society's association with the Cathedral through its organists meant that it gave regular concerts there continuing until the late 1980s, when the choir's name changed to 'The Bristol Chamber Choir'.

DECANI CANTORIS APPEAL

The Millennium Decani Cantoris Appeal (the terms Decani and Cantoris come from the different sides of the choir) was a fund-raising campaign to save the choral tradition of Bristol Cathedral Choir at its darkest hour when there were insufficient funds to implement its charitable purpose.

Music had been central to the life of the Cathedral and there had been an interrupted tradition of choral music stretching back at least 450 years to the reign of Henry VIII. Choristers had always been educated free of charge at Bristol Cathedral School. When the Direct Grant School was withdrawn in 1975, the choir was threatened, as this free education ceased. Six brave and farsighted individuals came up with a solution, and this heralded the creation of a Choral Foundation. A Trust Deed was signed on 6 October 1975 specifically to preserve choral worship and maintain the choral tradition in Bristol Cathedral by supporting the education of the choristers.

The foresight of the Trustees served them well, as they correctly predicted that, without the attraction of a free education, recruitment of Cathedral choristers would become increasingly difficult. This is precisely what happened. The six Founding Trustees subscribed for equal shares of £3 and thus the Foundation began with a capital sum of £18. The Founding Trustees were:

Peter Bale (a chorister parent and BBC wildlife producer)
Clifford Harker (the Organist and Master of Choristers)
Rev.Canon Evan Pilkington (a member of the Bristol Chapter)
The Reverend Anthony Bailey (The Succentor)
David Cannock (a local businessman)
Gerry Nichols (a former Head Chorister)

Bristol Cathedral's choral foundation was one of the earliest Choral Foundations amongst English cathedrals. However, the fund-raising was slow and painful, and the Trustees wisely decided that bursaries could only be met from income, not capital. It was therefore 15 years before sufficient capital had been raised to generate enough of an income stream to start making an active contribution to chorister school fees. In 1990, that work eventually began, and chorister parents received the active support of a bursary amounting to a third of school fees.

Over time, all the Founding Trustees, save David Cannock, left the Trust, and others joined. David Cannock became Chair until 1998 and was succeeded by Stephen Parsons, a former chorister. As the Millennium approached, it was clear that there was insufficient annual income generated by the Choral Foundation investments to influence chorister recruitment. More needed to be done, and Stephen Parsons evolved the idea of a Decani Cantoris Appeal to attract sufficient new funds to the Foundation. The challenge was to raise £74,000 over six years. Working with John Burke and the Cathedral Trust Office, a campaign was started and all ex-choristers were approached, together with musical trusts and corporate supporters. No stone was left unturned! The Appeal was successful and the Cathedral Choir was preserved in the short term – long enough for Bristol Cathedral School to become an Academy, when the education of choristers was once again free.

There were 16 major donors to the Decani Cantoris Appeal and their names are recorded on an oak board that hangs in the Song School.

THAT FUTURE CHORISTERS MAY EVER SING WITH
PERPETUAL JUBILATION SOME ONETIME CHORISTERS OF
BRISTOL CATHEDRAL GAVE MOST GENEROUSLY,
WITH OTHERS FROM AND BEYOND BRISTOL.

MILLENNIUM DECANI & CANTORIS APPEAL

DOROTHY BROWN
THE COMMANDERY OF SAINT BENEDICT
DAVID CANNOCK
MICHAEL DOSWELL
PAUL DYKE
LESLIE HARDWICK
CANON DAVID ISITT
JOHN JENKINS
BEA LEACH
SIMON LITTLEWOOD
DINAH MOORE
AILEEN MOON
STEPHEN PARSONS
LIONEL PIKE
THE JOHN PILLING TRUST
JEREMY WOOLF

THE VERY REVEREND ROBERT GRIMLEY	DEAN OF BRISTOL
HUGH MONRO	HEADMASTER
STEPHEN PARSONS	BRISTOL CATHEDRAL CHORAL FOUNDATION

(DB)

DEDICATION OF THE CHOIR STALLS, 1977

On Sunday, 25 September 1977 there was a Choral Evensong during which the Trustees of the Choral Foundation were present to witness the dedication of the Choristers' Stalls 'to the Glory of God' and in memory of:

Douglas Harrison
Cecil Rich
Michael Dyer
Graham Hooper
Percival Gay
Hubert Hunt
David Moon

A small brass plaque for each person was fixed on the stalls. These days their names are read, not only by casual passers-by in the choir area, but daily by the choristers themselves. Each and every one of those honoured had devoted a great part of their lives to the worship of the Cathedral and the education of its choristers.

Douglas Harrison – Dean, 1958-71. He greatly valued the choral tradition of the Cathedral and was keen to maintain its high standard.

Cecil Rich – Headmaster of the Cathedral School, 1946-70. For 24 years he constituted a drive for excellence, polish and exactitude in scholarship and manners.

Michael Dyer – The first official Assistant Organist, 1959-73. Accompanist also to Bristol Cathedral Special Choir as well as the Bristol Choral Society.

Graham Hooper – Organist of the Lord Mayor's Chapel, 1949-75.

He wrote a comprehensive history of Bristol's music.

Percival Gay – Honorary Canon, 1951-76. A lover of Bristol Cathedral's choral music and deeply concerned for the welfare of Lay Clerks and choristers.

Hubert Hunt – Organist and Master of the Choristers, 1901-45. It was for his work in the cause of cathedral music that the Archbishop of Canterbury conferred on him the Degree of DMus.

David Moon – Chorister, 1968-72, followed by serving as pupil Assistant Organist.

Since 1977, other brass plaques have been added that remember many associated with the worship and music of the Cathedral. They include Canons, Lay Clerks and benefactors as well as the names of one or two choristers who have died extremely young.

Cathedral choir stalls

59

OLD CHORISTERS' ASSOCIATION RE-FORMED

On a fine day in June 2011 we welcomed 'Old Choristers' of the newly re-formed Old Choristers Association (OCA) to Bristol Cathedral's first chorister reunion for decades. More than a year's preparation had gone into organising this event, with communications speeding all over the world in an effort to track down old friends. 'Boys' aged from 16 to 80 (some of whom had not met for 50 years) … and two 'girls' … greeted one another with surprise, delight and witty reminiscences before joining the current choristers for rehearsal.

The carefully chosen music for the event included favourite anthems, Parry's 'I was glad' and 'The Old Choristers' Anthem' by Hubert Hunt (Bristol Cathedral Organist until 1945), written especially for our Old Choristers' Association. Old and young sang together the Responses of Ayleward and the Magnificat and Nunc Dimittis setting in B flat by Stanford. Memory and technique flooded back and a tremendous sound was heard from the combined choir at that afternoon's Evensong. A new Old Choristers' badge was launched, which shows the circle of the Holy and Undivided Trinity surrounding the music of Bristol Cathedral. This is now given to choristers upon Valediction. Routine being all-important in the life of a cathedral, it is planned for the foreseeable future that the Old Choristers' Reunion should always take place on the Saturday before Sunday's Valediction.

Old Choristers' Evensong 2011

OLD CHORISTERS' MEMORIAL

Bristol Old Choristers' Association can prove to be a very good link back with the Cathedral for young people who travel the world and quite often settle in far-flung places. It is quite touching to see a memorial at the end of the cloister on the wall just before the entrance to the Cathedral doing precisely that same task nearly a century ago. This was erected on 15 May 1920, by the Cathedral's Old Choristers' Association, in memory of those Old Choristers who gave their lives in the Great War, 1914-18.

The memorial is constructed from a very colourful mosaic depicting a young classical warrior, looking remarkably like a boy chorister, with a sword and shield that is unashamedly patriotic – 'pro Patria' (for country) is emblazoned upon it. Over the warrior's head is written 'But yet there breaks a yet more glorious day', a clear quotation from the hymn 'For all the Saints', which was written as a processional hymn by the Anglican Bishop of Wakefield, William Walsham How. This is sung now, as it would have been then, on All Saints Day (1 November) and is instantly recognizable by choristers past and present.

morial at the
of the cloister

A few CDs drawn from a collection of many made by the
music department of the Cathedral

A Few Precedents

LIST OF EARLY PRECENTORS

FROM 1670

1	Francis Hanslape	1670 – 1686
2	James Taylor	1687 – 1711
3	Thomas Reed	1712 – 1716
4	Samuel Rogers	1716 – 1730
5	Robert Clarke	1730 – 1731
6	John Gregory	1731 – 1732
7	Robert Purcel	1732 – 1734
8	Thomas Gardner	1734 – 1739
9	Josiah Tucker	1739 –
10	William Packer	1780 – 1741
11	William Richard	1741 – 1755
12	John Camplin M.D.	1755 – 1782
13	Thomas Robins D.D.	1782 – 1790
14	John Camplin jun.	1790 – 1791
15	Owen Foster	1791 – 1792
16	Edward Bowles	1792 – 1793
17	James Brown	1793 – 1798
18	John Eden	1798 – 1799
19	Robert Foster	1799 – 1810
20	William Evan Dampier	1810 – 1812
21	Richard Bedford	1812 – 1817
22	Charles Baird	1824 – 1817
23	Joseph Cross	1825 – 1832
24	Henry Barker	1832 – 1838
25	Robert Llewellyn Caley	1838 – 1861
26	Alexander Neale	1861 – 1869
27	Frederick Charles Key	1869 – 1871

28	Edmund Renside Gregory	1871 – 1872
29	Charles Edward Key	1872 – 1882
30	William Lann	1882 – 1891
31	Edmund Renise Littlewis	1897 – 1910
32	Gerald James Ledington Lygan	1910 – 1913
33	Cyril Conley	1913 – 1917
34	George Madden Watkin	1917 – 1911
35	William Thomas Phillips	1911 – 1921
36	Jn. Mortimer D. Stancomb	1921 – 1928
37	William Frederick Ernest Pearith	1928 – 1936
38	Cyril Vincent Taylor	1936 – 1939
39	John Henry Williams	1939 – 1943
40	L. R. Perkins } Leonard William Guefold }	1943 – 1946
41	S.S.L. Swindells (Stanton Field Greenwood Swindells)	1946 – 1950
42	William Henry Bernard Houghton	1950 –

William Houghton 1950
Evan Pilkington 1968
David Isitt 1971
Jim Free 1982
John Rogan 1983
John Simpson 1989
Brendan Clover 1999
Wendy Wilby 2007

The Statutes of Bristol Cathedral demand that at the beginning of each year a Precentor is appointed alongside a number of other roles such as Vice-Dean and Archivist. This gives the flexibility for members of Chapter to change roles during their ministry at the Cathedral. In more recent times, priests have been installed as Canons Residentiary but with the understanding that they were appointed to fulfil the role of Precentor.

Amongst the collection of Bristol Cathedral archives held at Bristol Record Office is a beautifully handwritten book, its full title – *The Appeal of the Rev. Eccles James Carter, M.A. Minor Canon of the Cathedral Church* – set strikingly against its dark blue covers in gold letters, embossed on the spine. The volume gives a very full and detailed account of the appeal proceedings which followed Rev.

Bishop James Henry Monk

Carter's formal complaint against the then-Dean, Dr John Lamb, who had ordered that 'the portion of the service hitherto chanted in the Cathedral by the Minister shall … [from now on] be read'.

The Dean's order followed his appointment of the Rev. Sir Charles Macgregor, in 1848, as a Minor Canon, in spite of the fact that he was apparently unable to sing! To avoid any 'discord [that] may arise in the chanting' (from the Cathedral's Statute XXIII, concerning the role of the Precentor), the Dean, running roughshod over centuries-old tradition, twice decreed that those 'parts of the Liturgy … be read … in the Cathedral Church without any intonations or adding any thing in the matter or form thereto'. But there was absolutely no way that Rev. Carter was going to go along with this if he could help it. Minor Canons are employed specifically as 'singing men', and Carter protested that the Dean's suppression of the sung parts of Cathedral services ran counter to the oath that he had sworn on taking up his appointment.

Having garnered support from the Precentor, members of the Cathedral congregation and both Bristol's Mayor and Sheriff, his appeal was eventually heard by the Bishop, James Henry Monk, who declared the Dean's order 'to be null and void and of no validity whatsoever'. By November 1849, Sir Charles Macgregor had resigned, his position no longer tenable. We know that word of Carter's appeal spread widely as, soon afterwards, William Prendergast, Organist and Master of the Choristers at Winchester Cathedral, refers to it in a letter to *The Times* protesting at the curtailment of music within cathedrals.

THE MINOR CANON WHO COULD NOT SING PART 2

Bound into the front of Rev. Carter's handwritten volume is a long poem that satirises the whole affair between him and the Dean, Dr Lamb. Claiming to be 'a fragment of Rowley, unpublished by Chatterton', the poem playfully borrows the fictitious identity of monk Thomas Rowley, Bristol's controversial eighteenth-century poet Thomas Chatterton's medieval alter ego, and recasts the story within an imaginary medieval Bristol. Recounting the tale of the plucky 'clerk' who stood up for what he believed in, the poem delights in its thinly disguised ridicule of Dr Lamb. Chatterton's father had himself been a Minor Canon at Bristol Cathedral and, in one way, the poem might be taken as a celebration of the tradition, history and creativity of the Cathedral's musicians. Below you will find the first four verses of this humorous poem to give you the stylistic flavour. The jubilant final verse is added to show just how the saga ends!

Ye Bristowe mudde is fowle & blacke,
Ye Bristowe pathes uncleane;
But fylthyer wayes and pathes more fowle
Are trodde by Bristowe's Dene –

Ye Bristowe lanes are close & warme,
& Bristowe's walles are grimme,
Butte hotter & more darke ye berthe
Reserv'd I wot for himme –

Ane nobyll Lorde cam to ye Dene
And sayde to himme, says hee,
'I have a friende, whom thou must make
'Thy chorall clerke to bee –

'Of musycke knowes hee notte a note
'He chauntes in anie keye
'Yette notte for yatte mote yee rejecte
'A youthe of hye degree –'

Nowe lette us singe with loyall voice
Longe lyve owre gracyous Quene
And maye alle menne of evyll hertes
Be sarvyt lyke ye Dene. –

Ye Ende.

EDMUND FELLOWES, 1897-1900

The photograph you see of Edmund H. Fellowes and his wife, Lilian Hamilton, speaks to us of a bygone era, a time when the scholar-musician/cleric had an opportunity to flourish. Fellowes was born in Paddington, London, in 1870, and, after Winchester and then Oxford, he was ordained. He held a curacy in Wandsworth, after which he became Precentor of Bristol Cathedral in 1897, forming a lifelong friendship with the then Cathedral Organist, Percy Buck. These days in Bristol Cathedral were significant, formative and creative. He became a Minor Canon of St George's Chapel, Windsor for an astonishing 51 years – from 1900 to 1951 – and from 1924 to 1927 he was in charge of the choir following the death of the conductor Sir Walter Parratt.

Aided by Percy Buck, Edmund Fellowes brought about a revolution, albeit a gentle one: he both changed the way in which choral and other early music was understood and raised the quality of its performance within his own lifetime. Fellowes's passion for mid-sixteenth-century to mid-seventeenth-century music led him to edit 36 volumes of madrigals, 32 volumes of lute songs and 20 volumes of William Byrd's music, as well as a broad array of Tudor church music. His work covered not only the music, but also important biographical and critical writing such as *The English Madrigal Composers*, published in 1921, and *William Byrd*, published in 1936. According to Fellowes, 'the greatest thrill in the course of the whole of [his] researches' was finding Byrd's Great Service, which he stumbled upon while visiting Durham to complete some Gibbons anthems. As soon as he started transcribing the folio part-books he recognized that he had found 'a major work whose existence was till that moment unsuspected'.

Sixty-two years after his death, pretty much all we know about Edmund Fellowes comes from his autobiography, published in 1946 and modestly called *Memoirs of an Amateur Musician*. As a church musician, Fellowes recognized that what little Cathedral repertoire there was in his day was usually poorly performed. 'The interpretation of Tudor music began to force itself on my attention', he wrote. 'It became increasingly clear that rhythmic irregularity, as an essential feature of this music, was being generally unrecognized and ignored.'

Although once rather unkindly described as 'a stiff-necked Anglican clergyman', he was also quite a celebrity. A more sympathetic musical portrait of him comes from his younger contemporary Herbert Howells (1892-1983), who characterised him in the second movement – entitled 'Fellowes's Delight' – of his set of piano miniatures, 'Lambert's Clavichord', published in 1928.

67

GEORGE HOULDEN MERRIKIN, 1907-11

The story of George Merrikin is colourful and poignant. It describes a most difficult time at Bristol Cathedral and his early death as a distinguished hero in the Great War.

In the Chapter minutes of 1910-11, there are not many meetings which go by without reference to this Precentor, whose behaviour was giving cause for great concern. It all makes chilling reading. He was appointed in 1907, and already in May 1909 there were problems about his attendance at services. Clearly Merrikin felt that the members of the Chapter were bullies, and states that he was not prepared to be treated as a curate! Summoned before the Chapter and told in no uncertain terms that he was going to be expelled, Merrikin felt utterly humiliated and had to beg for money from his colleagues:

> The Precentor then asked that the sum of 5/- be allowed for his lunch: it was proposed by Canon Talbot and seconded by Archdeacon Robeson that the sum of 2/6 should be given the Precentor for lunch: the Clerk thereupon handed him that amount.

A few days later, the letter would have arrived at his house saying:

> That the Reverend George Houlden Merrikin be and is hereby expelled from his offices as Precentor and Minor Canon as from this day the 15th March 1911.

Born in 1878, Merrikin was Chaplain at Wellingborough School, Curate at Dulwich College and subsequently Precentor and Minor Canon at Bristol Cathedral. His time at the Cathedral terminated, in 1914 he enlisted as Private and Stretcher-bearer, Royal Army Medical Corps, eventually being posted to the Officer Cadet Battalion, Trinity College, Cambridge in October 1917. He was commissioned Second Lieutenant 1/2nd London Regiment in January

Revd. George Houlden Merrikin, expelled from the Cathedral

of 1918, joining his battalion in France on 29 April. He served with the battalion during the Second Battle of Arras and was killed in action on 27 August 1918. Military sources say that:

> under most heroic circumstances he met his death at a spot between Croisilles and Henin-sur-Cojeul, while going out in broad daylight to the German trenches to rescue eight or nine of our own wounded. He succeeded in saving eight men, and when going to save the last was shot through the heart.

He is buried in Summit Trench Cemetery, Croisilles, France. One can only imagine Merrikin's thoughts as he contrasted the traumatic reality and desperation of his serving soldiers with Trollopian cathedral life in Bristol.

68

WILLIAM THOMAS PHILLIPS, 1911-21

The Precentor who was appointed after the dismissal of the Reverend George Merrikin was William Thomas Phillips. Clearly ruffled by all that had happened, the Dean and Chapter were determined to make sure that the music of the Cathedral progressed without the mistakes of the recent past. They drew up some guidelines for their new Precentor, who was already serving as a Minor Canon at the Cathedral. These make very interesting reading from the perspective of the musical life of the Cathedral in the twenty-first century:

1. On offering the office of Precentor to the Rev. W.T. Phillips the Dean and Chapter hope that he will carry out a quiet but steady progressive work of reform. They specify such points as the following:

(a) Careful attention to the better order of the Choristers in the Cloisters and Vestry (this would include or imply being present in good time) – securing silence in entering and leaving the Cathedral. At present there is a considerable amount of chatter as they return to the Chapter House.

(b) Better behaviour on the part of the Lay Clerks. One member of the Choir takes his place without the semblance of kneeling for example. There is great room for improvement in reverence – proper silence in the service.

2. The Precentor must bestow time and pains on the whole question of the Lay Clerks' duties. Does the Precentor feel that he is prepared quite firmly and gently to hold a resolute ground as to the want of discipline and discontent among them? It will require patience, good temper and tact.

3. The Precentor must be very frequently in his stall, whether it

From Chapter minutes

is his rota for chanting or not. As the responsible musical officer of the Chapter he must be in the Cathedral on Sundays and constantly (not of course always) on weekdays. The Dean and Chapter consider this to be a matter on which the clearest understanding must exist.

4. Recognising the very great change that has come with modern times with the position of the organist, the Precentor would naturally consult with him on musical arrangements.

CYRIL VINCENT TAYLOR, 1936-9

No history of music in Bristol Cathedral would be complete without reference to Cyril Taylor's renowned hymn tune, 'Abbot's Leigh'. It was composed for the hymn 'Glorious things of thee are spoken' with words by the famous slave-ship owner turned abolitionist, John Newton. In more recent times this tune has also come to be used with many different texts, including 'Father Lord of all creation', 'God is here', 'Go my children, with my blessing' and 'Lord, you give the great commission'. It is found in the hymn books of most Christian denominations throughout the world.

Eric Routley writes of the tune as:

> The archetypal example of a hymn tune taught to the whole of Britain through broadcasting. Its secret, which gives it a sort of timeless authority that makes one feel as soon as one has heard it that one knew it all one's life, comes from the fact that its composer remembered what it was like to be in a pew singing.

Abbot's Leigh as a location has a significant place in the history of Bristol Cathedral, and Cyril would have been very familiar with that information. Robert Fitzharding (first Earl of Berkeley) acquired the village as Lord of the Manor and gave the income to the Abbey of St Augustine, Bristol, which he founded. At the dissolution of the Abbey, Morgan Gwilliam, the last Abbot, was awarded the Manor House at Abbot's Leigh. Here he lived in comfort with his orchard, garden and dovecote, plus 20 cartloads of wood and underwood for fuel each year – quite an incentive!

Born in 1907, Cyril Taylor was the son of an Anglican priest and, having gone up to Christ Church, Oxford, he was then ordained. He became Precentor of Bristol Cathedral from 1936 to 1939. During the Second World War, Cyril was the BBC's Producer of Religious Broadcasting, and it was during this time that he received such a volume of complaints about his choice of Haydn's

tune, 'Austria' (the German national anthem). He therefore composed his famous tune, 'Abbot's Leigh'. He was later involved in compiling the BBC Hymn Book, which was eventually published in 1951 (and to which, incidentally, he contributed some 20 tunes). Throughout his professional life he made a significant contribution to English church music.

About 'Abbot's Leigh', Dr Taylor, in a letter dated 21 March 1984, writes: 'to my great joy it has been sung at several great services, the last being that in Canterbury Cathedral (May 1983) in which the Archbishop and the Pope shared.'

Cyril Taylor died in 1991.

Stained-Glass Windows

70

KING DAVID PLAYING THE HARP IN THE EAST WINDOW

The great East Window of the Cathedral was constructed as part of the rebuilding of the chancel of the then-Abbey in the early 1300s. It is a wonderful example of the Decorated Gothic style of architecture. The story told by its glazed windows was reconstructed in the mid-1800s. This 'Jesse Window' illustrates the genealogy of our Lord, deriving its name from the biblical reference in Isaiah that 'a stem shall come out of the rod of Jesse'.

The legendary King David was Jesse's son, and his image appears, almost life size, in the fourth window from the right in the bottom row of figures. He is shown as a regal figure, bearded, wearing his crown and dressed in red with a white ermine collar. But the most noticeable feature of King David is the large harp that he appears to be playing with both hands. This ancient instrument, known in Hebrew as a 'kinnor', was widely used in the ancient world. It is, for example, mentioned several times as part of Nebuchadnezzar's orchestra in the third chapter of Daniel. It is actually more likely to be a lyre, although the words 'lyre' and 'harp' seem to be interchangeable in many biblical documents.

There are countless references to David in the Bible, and although famous for his victory over Goliath and as the second King of Israel, David's musical and poetic accomplishments are certainly well recorded. Known as 'the sweet psalmist of Israel' (2 Samuel 23.1), he is generally accredited or associated with 73 of the 150 Psalms. The Psalms are an essential part of almost all cathedral acts of worship, and are often sung by the choir. And so Psalms, being ancient songs with musical accompaniment, give us a direct and tangible link between the music and poetry of King David and our worship in the Cathedral in the twenty-first century.

Detail from East Window. (DB)

71

Angel Playing the Harp in the East Cloister

When the 11 windows of the East Cloister were reglazed as part of the post-war reconstruction of 1951, each window was dedicated to one of the important figures in the 399-year story of the Abbey. The main figures in the windows are of contemporary glass, supplemented by inserts of ancient glass recovered from previous glazing throughout the Cathedral building. Opposite the entrance to the chapter house is the window dedicated to Abbot Hunt, in which we find a fine piece of fourteenth-century glass portraying an angel playing a harp or lyre – an image that has become almost classical in the modern imagination.

Angels were never considered to be sexual and so our angel is shown as a beautiful androgynous being clothed in white and yellow, and playing a harp or lyre with both hands. (Here is another example of the word 'harp' and 'lyre' seeming to be interchangeable in many biblical documents.) Wings are shown, and there seems to be a halo around the yellow-haired head. Angels were also considered to be messengers of God, bringing not only good news, as at the Annunciation and the Birth and Resurrection of our Lord, but also bringing God's other gifts to humankind.

There are many references to harps and lyres throughout the Bible, especially in the Psalms, where the 12 references include injunctions to 'praise the Lord with a harp' (Ps 33.2) and 'praise him with the harp and lyre' (Ps 150.3), and the psalmists affirm 'I will praise you with the harp' on two occasions (Ps 43.4 & 71.22). The image of the angel offers us an insight into the medieval imagination, reflecting music's importance as part of God's gift to humankind.

Detail from window in Cloister

72

CHRIST IN MAJESTY (THE ROSE WINDOW)

Angel musicians are a common theme in the decoration of the Cathedral and form a helpful link between the medieval craftsmen and their Victorian counterparts. Both Choir Screen and High Altar Reredos date from the very end of the nineteenth century and employ large numbers of musicians of all types in their upper levels. The instruments shown are often based on those listed in the 150th Psalm, and care appears to have been taken to portray music as a richly colourful experience. Singers (usually holding banners used as musical scores) interact with a large 'broken consort' of players, based more on a sense of medieval variety than a nineteenth-century orchestral blend. The musical emphasis, like the Psalm, is clearly on the joyful rather than the religiose:

Praise him with the sound of the trumpet:
praise him with the psaltery and harp.
Praise him with the timbrel and dance:
praise him with stringed instruments and organs.
Praise him upon the loud cymbals:
praise him upon the high sounding cymbals.

Echoing this theme, but cast on a much grander scale, the Western Rose Window features 'Christ in Majesty' in its central panel surrounded by angels singing and playing an equally rich variety of instruments. Placed at a great distance from the centre, the outer ring portrays personifications of the Fine Arts, as practised by humankind, and features such endeavours as justice, navigation, welfare and industry.

Detail featuring angel musicians in Rose Window, west end. (DB)

Music in Stonework, Woodwork, Textiles and Art

STONE CARVING IN THE ELDER LADY CHAPEL

The Elder Lady Chapel remains one of the most attractive features of the Cathedral, especially with its lively stone carvings, not the least being an ape playing pan pipes and a ram playing a stringed instrument like a violin, possibly a rebec. The similarities with contemporary carvings in Wells Cathedral are obvious, and this connection can be confirmed by a letter from Abbot David's collection to the Dean of Wells asking him to lend his stone carver ('your servant L'). Abbot David was probably referring to Adam Lock, the Master Mason at Wells until 1229, and certainly there are parallels between the stonework at both cathedrals.

The humour of one age does not always appeal to that of another. Medieval wit can often be beyond us. We do nonetheless have something in common. William Hazlitt pointed out that the basis of all humour lies in the juxtaposition of two seemingly disconnected elements. So in these carvings we perceive the humour of animals not only being able to play musical instruments but also in a church, too. There could be a double entendre here – an ape imitates a human and people imitate others; in modern parlance they 'ape someone'. Certainly down the ages there has often been a critical interplay between monkeys and humans. With the ram comes the same sort of innuendo, but this time connecting the rampant activity of the animal with the lusts of the male. If G.C. Coulton was right in thinking that the constant problem of monasteries was how to keep women out, then this carving is a reminder to the Augustinian Canons of their commitment to chastity!

Ram and monkey playing instruments, Elder Lady Chapel. (DB)

ANGEL MUSICIANS IN THE CHOIR STALLS

The finely carved choir stalls were made for the Abbey Church during the time that Robert Elyot was Abbot (1515-25). Their flamboyant designs depict intertwined naturalistic foliage. Various legendary creatures featured include those in the arms of the Berkeley family, who continued to be generous benefactors to the Abbey. The initials and arms of Abbot Elyot also appear, in more than a dozen places. The misericords beneath the choir seats are notable for their depictions of daily life and popular fables such as the stories of Reynard the Fox, Bruin the Bear and Tybert the Cat. At the ends of each row of stalls are carvings of angels playing musical instruments. Some have harps and one plays a wind instrument that is probably a shawm. Other instruments include cymbals and a small portative organ; there are seated angels playing plucked string instruments that are likely to represent citterns.

The size of the choir stalls and the quality of the carving is a reminder of the importance of music and of the choral accompaniment to the services in the Abbey Church. This is evident from the surviving Abbey account rolls for the period. The detailed Latin accounts for 1511-12 show payments to Richard Bramston, or Brampeston, who was Master of the Choristers (see entry no. 7). He had been a Vicar Choral at Wells Cathedral and had come to St Augustine's Abbey in c.1510. He received an annual stipend of £3 6s 8d, as well as board and lodging in the Abbey. There were four choirboys who spent much of their time in the Elder Lady Chapel and are described in the accounts as 'the boys of the Chapel of the Blessed Mary'. They were lodged in the Almonry. As well as being given 'bread, ale, meat, fish and other victuals' for himself and the boys, Richard Bramston also received '34 yards of woollen cloth of violet colour' for the boys' cassocks.

An earlier account shows that 20 ells of blood-coloured woollen cloth were purchased for the four boys of the Lady Chapel. On the feast of St Nicholas (6 December) each year 12d was spent on presents for the choirboys. For important services their singing would have been supplemented by the voices of the novices and some of the Canons. In c.1515 Richard Bramston returned to Wells Cathedral, where he became Master of the Choristers. He was an accomplished musician, and two of his settings are still extant: the five-part antiphon 'Marie Virginis fecunda viscera' and 'Recordare domine Testamenti tui'.

The Augustinian Abbey possessed an organ that was to survive the dissolution of the Monastery in 1539 and was used for several years in the Cathedral. It is evident from manuscript decoration and late medieval carvings in other churches that wind, string and percussion instruments, as well as organs, provided enrichment for the liturgy. The angel carvings on the Bristol choir stalls make it probable that other instruments were used in the Abbey, but, sadly, the surviving account rolls do not mention them.

Wood carving in the choir stalls. (DB)

WALL PAINTING FROM THE OLD DEANERY

In a space which used to be the dormitory passage and is now a sacristy, some enigmatic wall paintings are displayed. These feature scriptural figures and episodes and a number of emblems, one of which includes the Latin tag, *Secreta mea mihi* ('My secrets are mine'). The paintings were rescued from the Old Deanery prior to its demolition. They were found under wallpaper when Dean Lamb was in office in the 1840s, in a place which previously could well have been a dormitory for boys, maybe choristers. They were then displayed in the temporary Cathedral Museum, close to where they are stored now.

It is possible that the paintings date from c. 1580 to the early 1600s. George Pryce, who had been Bristol City Librarian, took great interest in them when they were discovered and copied them. He described them as being 'depicted in clear black outline without colour or shading' which points to them being grisailles (works in grey or grey-black monochrome). Grisaille-work certainly held some popularity as a technique for wall paintings in England from the late fifteenth century. Almost certainly the black pigment is charcoal or lampblack and water-based, bound with gum. The Bristol paintings are outline drawings and do not set out to imitate nature in terms of conventional three-dimensionality. This technique is entirely appropriate to the allegorical material of the scheme. The pictures appear to be painted onto plaster fixed to a support of wooden struts. The frieze, it is suggested, was created for an audience of adolescent boys who may well have been familiar with acting. It is the case that the famous boy-actor companies of the time comprised boy choristers (for example, the boys of Magdalen school in Oxford and the St Paul's choristers in London).

A possible source for the texts may have been musical. Part of the Magnificat appears and there are short snatches taken from the Psalms and the Epistles that may well have been set musically. *Sanctus Spiritus*, which is repeated three times, has a musical ring

to it as well – all this could point to the boy choristers again, who would have appreciated and understood the paintings in the dormitory. Further information can be found in Catherine Oakes' chapter in *The Medieval Art, Architecture and History of Bristol Cathedral: An Enigma Explored*, edited by Jon Cannon and Beth Williamson.

BENEDICITE

Hidden round the corner in the vestibule of the Berkeley Chapel is a large roundel, a painting that has *Ave Maria* inscribed on its circular frame. If you look carefully you will see six beautiful young angels surrounding the Madonna and Child, and two of them are playing instruments. One in a green dress plays the lute, with her eyes closed in spiritual ecstasy, and another carries a lyre or a small harp in her left hand, but she is bending forward eagerly to view the infant Jesus. Such instruments are typically seen in Pre-Raphaelite paintings.

The canvas was painted by William Titcomb during a visit to Florence in 1904 and is unlike his normal style. It was clearly inspired by the religious masterpieces he could see around him, even to the upright cypresses in the background that you can spot everywhere in Tuscany. This painting is also somewhat reminiscent of the English Pre-Raphaelite, Thomas Cooper Gotch, whose naturalistic style of art threw away the rules and conventions that were drilled into students' heads at the art academies.

The Madonna herself was modelled by the children's nanny, Nurse Ethel Dickinson, who later became a nun and adopted the name Sister Etheldreda. The young angel on the right holding a carnation was modelled on the artist's daughter, Loveday, whom he painted a number of times.

William Titcomb had moved to Bristol in 1909 and was already a highly regarded artist. The education of his children was paramount for him and his wife, Jessie. They had previously moved to Düsseldorf in 1905 for the children's schooling but, with the rise of nationalism in Germany, returned to England. Will taught art at Clifton High School and joined the Bristol Savages straightaway, where he enjoyed the convivial company of fellow artists. Nowadays the Bristol Savages still functions as a club for male artists ('red feathers'), though performing musicians are also allowed to become members as part of the 'entertainers' group ('blue feathers').

Roundel hung near the Berkeley Chapel. (DB)

A seat cushion worked by one of the embroiderers of the Cathedral. It echoes the stone carving in the Elder Lady Chapel. Thre are many more cushions and kneelers made by members of the Cathedral community

ICONS OF ST JORDAN AND ST AUGUSTINE

The Feast of the Holy Trinity in 2010 not only saw a new Dean installed in Bristol Cathedral but also the dedication of a newly commissioned pair of icons. These can now be seen in the Elder Lady Chapel, where people light candles and pray in front of the images of St Jordan of Bristol and St Augustine of Canterbury.

It is thought that Jordan was one of the 30 monks and priests who, with about 10 more missionaries, set off from Rome with Augustine in AD 597. Their trip to Bristol came about because of a conference in AD 603 which was designed to bring to heel the bishops of the unreformed post-Roman British Church in the western part of our island. Here the bishops were obdurate and unyielding in their opinions and, frankly, not too happy about receiving instructions from Rome.

St Jordan has long been accepted in the Bristol tradition as the junior colleague of St Augustine. He was his trusted companion and former student, and it is thought that he was left behind in Bristol to further the work of evangelism in this place, eventually dying here and being laid to rest in a chapel that was dedicated to him on the Green. That, of course, is a happy speculation, but the presence of a chapel dedicated to Jordan is certainly well documented and can be clearly seen on Jacob Millerd's map dating from 1673.

Musically we must turn to a hymn to St Jordan in a Book of Hours which can now be found in Sidney Sussex College, Cambridge. This devotional book once belonged to a Bristolian, and it is believed that it could have been used in St Jordan's Chapel dating way back to about 1450. From the hymn to St Jordan found in this Horae we learn that the oratory of St Jordan on the Green was indeed his mausoleum:

Ad honorem dei et sancti Jordani
O felix Christi confessor concivis caeli Jordane
Sis pro fide intercessor nostre gentis anglicane
Quam in fide perfecisti Augustino baptizante

Cui consors extitisti ipso anglis predicante.
Huius loci patronus in quo iaces tumulatus …

To the Honour of God and St Jordan
O Jordan, blessed confessor of Christ and citizen of Heaven
Intercede for us by virtue of the faith we of the English church pro-
fess
Whom Augustine baptised and you perfected in that holy trust
Whose colleague you were in his preaching to the English.
Be our patron in this place where you lie entombed …

This hymn would no doubt have been chanted alongside the other
Psalms, litanies and antiphons of the day. In present times we
have adapted it slightly to fit a traditional plainsong hymn chant,
and this is occasionally sung in the Cathedral:

St Jordan's Hymn

From the Book of Hours of St Jordan's Chapel (ascr 1450)

O Fe - lix Chri - sti Con - fe - ssor con - ci - vis Cae - li Jor - da - ne, Sis

pro fi - de in - ter - ce - ssor nos - tre gen - tis an - gli - ca - ne Quam in fi - de per - fec - is - ti Au

gu - sti - no bap - ti - zan - te Cu - i con - cors ex - ti - tis - ti ip - so an - gles pre - di - can - te, Hu -

ic lo - ci sis pa - tro - nus in quo ia - ces tu - mu - la - tus

Icons of St Jordan and St Augustine in the Elder Lady Chapel

The Cathedral School

A ROYAL VISIT TO THE CATHEDRAL, 1574

Many stirring scenes have been witnessed in Bristol in connection with visits of royal personages, but the one of which we possess the most quaint and interesting record is the visit of Queen Elizabeth I to this city and its Cathedral Church in the course of one of her royal 'progresses'.

On 14 August 1574, 'Good Queen Bess' arrived at the city of Bristol, and at the High Cross, which then stood at the junction of the four central streets of the ancient city, she was addressed by 'an excellent boye, disguised as Faem'. Afterwards, at St John's Gate, at the bottom of Broad Street, she was addressed by three other boys, 'disguised as Salutacion, Gratulacion, and Obedient Goodwill'. It is highly probable that these 'excellent boyes' were cathedral schoolboys. It was quite a tradition in England for royalty to be greeted by people dressed up in all sorts of unusual costumes.

In 1575, Thomas Churchyard published a book called *Churchyarde's Chippes*. We learn from the book this information:

> The Sunday next the Queene went to the colledge, to hear a sarmond, whear thear was a speech to be sayd, and an imme was songe; the speetch was left out by an occasion unlooked for, but the imme was songe by a very fien boye.

The 'fien boye', surely a chorister, and his schoolmates doubtless had a good time during the two or three days following the Queen's visit to the Cathedral – a period in which, for the entertainment of Her Majesty, the lands of the Dean and Chapter on both sides of the river (as well as the river itself) were set aside for the enactment of several mock battles.

CHORISTERS IN THE EIGHTEENTH CENTURY

In 1913, Edwin Thomas Morgan, a Lay Clerk at the Cathedral, wrote the first *History of the Bristol Cathedral School* ever published. In addition to this, in the Bristol Records Office resides a catalogue of the Muniments of Bristol Cathedral that he compiled. This work he began in October 1911 and completed in August 1912. In the preface of his book, E.T. Morgan explains that the Dean and Chapter allowed him to have access to many interesting

Choristers at play

Cathedral records that were supposed to have been destroyed in the riots of 1831. This conscientious and historically aware musical gentleman has left for us in his book an excellent and unique picture of the lives of the choristers in times gone by.

Boys seem to have been boys at all times, and we are not very much surprised to find, under the date 24 July 1780, that:

Complaints having been made of the misbehaviour of the Choristers during Divine Service, it is ordered that a book entitled
Merrick's *Translation of the Psalms* be kept in the vestry, and that
any Chorister so misbehaving shall be confined to the vestry from
the time of Morning Prayer to the Evening Prayer of the same day.
And that he have a portion of one of the said Psalms given him to
be learned by heart, not less than 20 lines, and not more than 30
at one time. And if he shall neglect or refuse to learn them during
his first confinement, then his confinement shall be repeated in
the same manner day after day till he repeat his task perfectly.
And if he shall wilfully spoil or deface the book, the Chapter Clerk
shall provide another, and pay for it out of the Sallary of the Chorister so offending.

It is staggering to look at this punishment for choristers from the
eighteenth century in the light of current safeguarding in the Music
Department of the Cathedral!

81

TRAGEDY STRIKES A NINETEENTH-CENTURY CHORISTER

I think it would be true to say that the Cathedral school buildings
have always been a logistical challenge to the Dean and Chapter,
probably even up to the time when the government-funded Academy opened in 2008. In the mid-nineteenth century, considerable
alterations were made in the school accommodation in the cloisters, and provision was also made for dormitories for prospective
boarders.

On 30 November 1867, however, a most distressing accident
happened at the schoolhouse. I suppose in these litigious days,
'Health and Safety' checks might well have prevented this, but,
tragically, the result was the death, three days later, of Francis
Scott Gray, a chorister and son of one of the Lay Vicars of St
Patrick's Cathedral, Dublin. According to the evidence given at the

Coroner's Inquest, which was held on 4 December, the lad, who was aged 11 years and 9 months, attempted to slide down the banisters of the staircase, though he had previously been warned not to do so. Missing his hold, he fell into the hall below, a depth of 20-30 feet, fracturing his skull and sustaining other serious injuries. The jury returned a verdict of 'Accidental Death'. On the same day his funeral took place in the churchyard attached to the Cathedral. The Lay Clerks and choristers attended and sang the service and also a chorale at the graveside. There is a memorial cross over his grave near the Berkeley Chapel.

Memorial cross on the chorister's grave

| BURIALS in the ~~Parish of~~ Cathedral Church & Churchyard in the County of ~~of~~ City of Bristol in the Years 1867 | | | | |
Name.	Abode.	When buried.	Age.	By whom the Ceremony was performed.
Francis Scott Gray (killed by a fall from the banisters) No. 369. (a chorister)	College Grammar School	Dec 5th 1867	11 Yrs	Alex. Poole (Precentor)
John Middleton (Esquire)	Clifton No. 6. Gloucester	April 11th 1868	96 Yrs	David And Bishop ...

From the Cathedral burial register

The refoundation of a Henrician Choir School of 1542 was a great moment in its history, and all the more so as teaching and learning had been happening at St Augustine's Abbey since the end of the twelfth century. That continuum of almost a thousand years came perilously close to coming to an end in 2007 as Bristol Cathedral School struggled to attract sufficient fee-paying pupils to balance its books. The Cathedral Choir was then reduced to just 12 choristers and recruitment was difficult. It was almost possible to predict the last Choral Evensong with the Cathedral Choir, and thus the end of the choral tradition in Bristol Cathedral, as we knew it, was on the horizon.

In this bleak midwinter of 2007, Frank Field MP published an article on Christmas Eve in *The Sunday Times* entitled 'The Silence of the Choirs'. In it he described the challenge that a typical Dean and Chapter throughout the UK was facing and at the same time offered a solution, which was to convert independent choir schools into government-funded Academies. The Dean of Bristol at that time, the Very Rev. Robert Grimley, was extremely supportive of this idea, as were the Deans' Conference and the Association of English Cathedrals. The Governors, led by the Chairman, Stephen Parsons, and supported by the Precentor, Canon Wendy Wilby, also saw this as a tailor-made solution to the problems of Bristol Cathedral School. Twenty-one months later, Bristol Cathedral School became Bristol Cathedral Choir School and opened as an Academy in September 2008.

Following a massive financial investment, wonderful new teaching facilities had been created on the south side of College Square, including an IT capability fit for the twenty-first century. The final touch was provided by the stonemasons of Stokes Masonry Ltd of Bath, who carved the name Bristol Cathedral Choir School with pride. That hand carving of letters with hammer and chisel was so symbolic of what was being achieved in the reded-

icated Choir School. Stonemasonry has changed little since the twelfth century, rather like choral worship. School fees were abolished and BCCS became an independent Academy with a music and maths specialism. Since 2008, the Academy has almost doubled in size to 700 pupils and the choir has grown to about 36 girl and boy choristers each year, with 16 probationers.

Thus, the Cathedral's choral tradition was saved once more, and Bristol has a great new city-centre school founded upon a musical heritage that stretches way back to Plantagenet England. In a strange way, everything had to be changed for everything to stay the same.

WILLIAM CHILD (MUSICAL ALUMNUS)

William Child was born in Bristol in 1606 and was a chorister in the Cathedral under Elway Bevin. In 1630 he began a lifetime association with St George's Chapel, Windsor, first becoming a Lay Clerk, and then, in 1632, being appointed one of the organists and Master of the Choristers. That same year he was also appointed one of the organists of the Chapel Royal. In 1643, at the dissolution of the Chapel, Child retired to a farm in the country, where he continued to compose music such as the anthem, 'O Lord, grant the King a long life', which would not have endeared him to the Puritans – nor indeed were there many years left for Charles I!

At the Restoration of the Monarchy in 1660, Child was present at the Coronation of Charles II, was reappointed to St George's Chapel and was made a Gentleman of the Chapel Royal and also Master of the King's Wind Music. One of his most popular compositions, reprinted three times during his lifetime, was a set of 20 short anthems for two trebles and bass, with words taken from the Psalms. There are also 17 service settings among the church music and a certain amount of secular music, including catches and instrumental pieces.

Church and cathedral organists have often been at variance with their respective clergy and Chapters. Child at one point made a rather amusing bargain with his employers:

Dr Child having been organist for some years to the King's Chapel in King Charles 2nd's time had great arrears of salary due to him, to the value of about

£500, which he and some of our canons discoursing of, Dr C. slited [sic], and said he would be glad if anybody would give him £5 and some bottles of wine for; which the canons accepted of, and accordingly had articles made with hand and seal. After this, King James 2nd coming to the crown, paid off his Brs. arrears; whch much affecting Dr Child, and he repining at, the canons generously released his bargain, on condition of his paving the body of the choir wth. marble, wch. was accordingly done, as is comemorated [sic] on his gravestone.

William Child died in his 91st year and is buried in St George's Chapel. He had been an influential musician in a difficult period for church music, and is yet another example of the many church musicians over the last 400 years who owed their training and indeed their profession to Bristol Cathedral.

DENNIS NOBLE (MUSICAL ALUMNUS)

Amongst all the musicians connected with Bristol Cathedral it is fitting to have the success story of a boy who was trained by Dr Hubert Hunt and who became perhaps the most well-known English baritone of his day. This boy was William Ewart Noble, born in Bristol in 1898. He studied under Dr Hunt at the Bristol Cathedral Choir School.

Invalided during war service in France, he nevertheless returned to the front to sing with the Fifth Army's entertainment unit. After the war, when he decided to turn professional, he chose the name Dennis Noble. He joined the Choir of Westminster Abbey and sang at the wedding of the Duke of York (later King George VI) and Lady Elizabeth Bowes-Lyon in 1923. Soon he was singing leading roles in opera at Covent Garden, although he also always enjoyed singing in musical comedy. In 1931 he was the baritone soloist in the first performance of Sir William Walton's 'Belshazzar's Feast',

Dennis Noble

a work which he recorded twice. He sang in many other world premières, none equalling the success of the Walton.

In the 1940s he could be heard singing in 'La Traviata' with Joan Hammond and 'The Barber of Seville' with Heddle Nash, recording 'The Dream of Gerontius' with Sir Malcolm Sargent, and also appearing in *1066 and All That* with Michael Redgrave and Ivor Novello.

He was renowned for his enunciation and his diction and for the almost metallic quality of his voice – the result of the excellent training he had received from Dr Hunt, which enabled him to succeed in opera, oratorio, musical comedy and song for over 40 years. He died in 1966, aged 67.

RUSS CONWAY (MUSICAL ALUMNUS)

Most cathedral choirs can point to one or two of their number who eventually become musicians of some repute, but Trevor Herbert Stanford turned out to be quite a surprising star and a household name to many – the legendary Russ Conway. Born on 2 September 1925 in Bedminster, Trevor played the piano throughout his childhood despite only managing to survive one piano lesson! His innate musical talent enabled him to win a scholarship to Bristol Cathedral School to sing in the choir, but he had left school by 14 and soon ended up in borstal for stealing. Loving the sea, as do so many Bristolians, his rather chequered career took him into the Merchant Navy and eventually the Royal Navy during the Second World War, when he was rewarded with a Distinguished Service Medal for 'gallantry and devotion to duty'.

After the War he was soon back playing in pubs and bars, but it wasn't really until 1957, when he accompanied Dorothy Squires on the variety bill at the Metropole Theatre in London, that his keyboard career took off – and what a success it was! Many of us can remember the number-one record 'Side Saddle', which lasted 30 weeks in the charts. It led to a decade of familiar piano-tinkling activity with many hit records, such as 'Roulette' and 'China Tea', and regular appearances on Billy Cotton's weekly variety show as well as three Royal Variety Performances.

Russ Conway

Russ Conway was one of Britain's biggest-selling music artists before The Beatles, with sales of 30 million records, but his career came to a premature halt when he suffered a stroke in 1965. By the early 1970s he was, by his own admission, 'becoming difficult to work with'.

Drinking heavily and addicted to anti-depressants, he went from considerable wealth to near-bankruptcy. With the support of his show-business friends, eventually he climbed back onto an even keel to work again, but on a much smaller scale around the country in summer seasons. Russ Conway died in 2000.

HERBERT CHAPPELL (MUSICAL ALUMNUS)

Over the years the Cathedral Choir School has been blessed with its fair share of 'natural' musicians who went on to achieve considerable success. One such pupil was Herbert Chappell. Born in 1934, he first began to compose whilst still a Cathedral chorister at Bristol. He studied with Clifford Harker and gained a place at Oxford University. Here he attended absolutely no lectures after his first week – not unusual amongst the Oxford student population of course! However, he spent much of his time composing musicals and incidental music for amateur theatrical productions, which proved to be just the right grounding required for his future career. With an abundance of natural talent, he achieved a first-class degree and went on to complete a BMus before beginning an unfinished DPhil in orchestration.

Leaving academia behind him, Chappell joined the ranks of London's freelance composers. That was the moment, he says, when he suddenly found himself writing for studio musicians, and his real education began. He scored and conducted everything from advertising jingles to feature films such as *Licensed to Kill*. He was to compose more than 250 scores for TV plays and for series such as 'The Pallisers', as well as the ever-popular 'Paddington Bear' narrated by Stephen Fry, which appeals to children and adults alike. Many from his generation will also remember his original theme tune for BBC's 'Songs of Praise'.

For children, amongst other compositions, he had great success with 'The Daniel Jazz' as well as 'Dead in Tune', a musical 'whodunnit' for a narrator and the Leicestershire Schools Orchestra, to introduce young children to the different orchestral instruments.

Wearing a different hat, he has written and directed many award-winning music documentary films for television. Chappell's prize-winning film of 'African Sanctus' introduced choirs and audiences in many countries to the music of David Fanshawe. His glorious production of the original 'Three Tenors' concert from

Rome, during the 1990 World Cup, was televised live to 56 countries and to an estimated 800 million viewers, and has been somewhat responsible for attracting an ever-expanding audience of classical music-lovers.

GARETH MORRIS (MUSICAL ALUMNUS)

Gareth Morris was born in Clevedon and came to Bristol Cathedral School in 1931, when he was 11. He loved the Cathedral and was much affected by the beauty of the building and of its services and music. He was not, however, an enthusiastic pupil: he did not enjoy being told what to read and do, and he contrived to leave without taking any exams or playing much part in the life of the school. The problem was that he had decided at the age of 10 what his future was to be and he was single-minded in pursuing his course. On discovering a fife in an old trunk, and learning how to play it, he determined to be a professional musician. He badgered the conductor of the Clevedon Silver Band until he was allowed to join it. Summers spent on the bandstand, playing from parts written for other instruments, gave him an excellent grounding in sight-reading and transposition. He graduated to lessons in London with Robert Murchie, principal flute of the BBC Symphony Orchestra, and when he was 18 won a scholarship to the Royal Academy of Music.

While still a student, he was asked to play in the 'St Matthew Passion' with the great oboist Leon Goossens and his career began in earnest. Soon after the Second World War, spent with the RAF Symphony Orchestra, he became principal flute in Walter Legge's newly founded Philharmonia Orchestra and played under a glittering array of conductors – Furtwängler, Toscanini, Klemperer and Karajan among them. He also returned to the Royal Academy of Music as Principal Professor of the Flute; he loved teaching and continued there for 40 years, always ensuring that he made time for it in spite of many playing commitments. He

Gareth Morris

joined his great friend, the horn player Dennis Brain, in his wind quintet, Evelyn Rothwell in her Wind Trio, and numerous ad hoc orchestras and film sessions.

His playing career was ended by a violent mugging in New York during a tour with the Philharmonia Orchestra. However, he refused to be depressed by this, retaining his optimistic, affectionate and very amusing character – the fierce frown being the result of a sightless eye and not of a furious temper! He continued to teach at the Royal Academy of Music until his retirement in 1985, when he moved to Bristol, and then carried on adjudicating and teaching privately until his death in 2007. His funeral service was held in the Cathedral which he loved, and he is buried in Clevedon, where it all began.

Odds and Ends

'ODDS AND ENDS' BY DEAN FRANCIS PIGOU

'Sitting over my fire one October evening, wondering, as I had wondered years ago in my first curacy, if God would call me to any higher work in His Church, my wife said to me: 'If God were to say to you, "Ask what I shall give thee" what would you ask for?' I replied: "Send me to Bristol".'

Thus begins the final chapter of Pigou's autobiography, *Phases of My Life*. This colourful and eminent priest had moved from being Vicar of Halifax Parish Church to Chichester Cathedral where he served as Dean for three years; but it was in 1891 that he was offered the Deanery at Bristol, the Cathedral of his dreams, and here that he finally died in 1916, being buried in his chosen spot – the Cathedral garden directly outside the Berkeley Chapel.

We would be so much the poorer without Pigou's two books *Phases of My Life* and *Odds and Ends*, which has an ebullient chapter on 'Cathedrals and Cathedral Life'. The content of this chapter overflows with musical stories and irrepressible humour. He takes time within it to write about all the different roles in the Cathedral, especially those of the Music Department and Choir. Having dealt with Precentors, Organists and Minor Canons, he then turns his sardonic pen to Lay Clerks:

Lay Clerks have tricks, not to speak of whispering and unnecessary communication with each other; there are sadly listless attitudes; singing with folded arms; not kneeling when they ought to kneel; not bowing the head when they should bow it; not reciting the Creed; looking over music during the reading of the lessons, studying the anthem when presumably joining in prayer, and divers sundry and other 'tricks'. I could sometimes wish that a sine qua non should be that a lay clerk should not wear a moustache, or at least that he dispense with it on Sundays! All who are thus decorated do not offend in this particular, but exercise self-restraint; but oh! what an instrument of unrighteousness a moustache is in some cases! How it lends itself to 'twiddling' and perpetually feeling if it is there! Such details as these may appear insignificant, not worth being noticed, but I sometimes think if a 'snapshot' could be taken of a choir during Divine service it would show, when 'developed', that they are by no means insignificant details and such as might be discontinued.

Memorial to Dean Pigou in the nave. (DB)

THOMAS CHATTERTON'S ACCOUNT

In and amongst the hundreds of files and boxes which make up the Cathedral's collection of archives, is a single sheet of paper mottled brown with age and about A5 in size. Its title, in neat hand-writing, still clearly legible, is 'An Account of the Music written in the Books belonging to the Cathedral Church of Bristol from the 9th of January 1748 to the 9th of June 1750 – with additional paper'. Listed line-by-line underneath is the name of each of the Minor Canons and the number of sides of music, together with any additional sheets which had been copied into their books, next to a sum of money. 'In Mr Dines Book', for example, there were 10 Sides & 7 Sheets for 10½d.

Although music was being printed at this time, the document tells us that music was still being copied out by hand into each of

Chatterton House

the books used by the Cathedral Choir. Of course, the copying would need to be carefully done – any mistakes might result in some peculiar, discordant noises – and the precise manner in which the Account itself has been compiled suggests that its compiler may also have been responsible for undertaking such work.

The Account has been signed off: 'Received the 26 June 1750 of Mr. James Purnell Deputy Treasurer the full contents of this note by me Thomas Chatterton.' This Thomas Chatterton is the father of his celebrated namesake, the wayward Bristol poet who was to be such an influence on a later generation of poets including Southey, Coleridge, Wordsworth and Keats. Our Chatterton died before his son was born, but we know that he was one of the Minor Canons at Bristol Cathedral for some time, as his name appears in the Cathedral's quarterly pay sheets from 1748. And if, as we might suppose, it was Chatterton himself who undertook the copying work, it would no doubt have provided a useful supplement to his income.

DESTRUCTION OF THE MUSIC LIBRARY, 1831

In 1831, as part of the protests against the Reform Act, a mob of several hundred rioters attempted to burn down many prominent buildings throughout the city. Although they were finally defeated in their attempt to burn the Cathedral itself, much was lost, including the Bishop's Palace and the historic music library. We may assume that the greater part of the collection was handwritten and was often contained in individual part-books. The loss of an individual voice part all too often rendered the whole composition unperformable. Although little music has survived, we do have some financial documentation that is preserved in the Records Office, and we can glean a little of the choir's eighteenth-century repertoire from this incomplete catalogue.

The use of handwritten copies of music had clearly provided a limited income for certain local musicians for many years.

The Burning of the Bishop's Palace, 1831, WJ Müller.
Courtesy of Bristol's Museums Galleries and Archives

However, the growth of printed copies in full scores became much more preferable, as a bill dated 27 December 1808, can testify.

It is signed by John Wasbrough, who served as Organist between the years 1807 and 1825. Wasbrough's successor was John Davis Corfe, who was Organist for 51 years between 1825 and 1876 and would have been responsible for rebuilding the Cathedral's music after the riot. This bill suggests that printed music was now the norm and that multiple copies of Boyce's *Cathedral Music* formed the staple diet of the new regime.

91

'MESSIAH' AND DEAN HORACE DAMMERS

Bristol Cathedral's association with Handel's 'Messiah' dates from the occasion of its first ecclesiastical performance in August 1758 when, in spite of public reservations, the Dean and Chapter finally allowed 'Messiah' to be performed for the first time in a Cathedral Church. Wherever the Gospel is preached, and wherever the English language is understood, Handel's unforgettable musical images preach more clearly than 10,000 sermons. Amongst those present was John Wesley, who recorded in his Journal:

> Thursday 17th August 1758
> I went to the Cathedral to hear Mr. Handel's Messiah. I doubt if that congregation was ever so serious at a sermon as they were during this performance. In many places, especially several of the choruses, it exceeded my expectation.

In a more recent age, Dean Horace Dammers wrote his last extended meditation on Handel's masterpiece. Published posthumously, the Dean takes us through the libretto, offering us a thought-provoking interpretation of the biblical references for his own time and a model for the future. He ends with the text of Handel's final chorus:

> Blessing, and honour, glory, and power, be unto him that sitteth upon the throne, and unto the Lamb, for ever and ever. Amen. (*Rev.* 5.12, 13)

If blessing is a very significant word, then Amen is perhaps the most significant word there is in English or any language. So I am glad that Handel gives it such elaborate treatment. For Amen (so be it) commits the man or woman who prays it. Most of us have little enough power to change the world. But there is one area

In the Cathedral garden. (DB)

over which, unless we ourselves are very poor, we have control;
and that is our own life style … live simply that all may simply live.

The very last sentiment above was Dean Dammers' watchword,
and his life and ministry testify to this vision.

92

PRECENTOR'S SUMMER MUSIC FESTIVAL

Josephine Goddard

Over the last few years the Cathedral has opened its doors to visitors for its Festival of Summer Music. Running independently from the annual concert series run by the Director of Music, the series was designed to fill a space in the Cathedral's outreach and welcome at a time when its own musicians were on annual leave.

The idea, which sprang originally from a desire to promote the Cathedral as a centre of culture, flourished under the oversight of Canon John Simpson, who joined the staff as Precentor in 1989. Originally, Simpson had served in the Navy, and he gained the reputation of being the only person to have taken a harpsichord below the waves in a submarine. During his time in Bristol he was also Chairman of Bristol Cathedral Concerts Ltd, the Bristol and Swindon Area of the Royal School of Church Music, and a member of the Bristol City Tourism Committee. The series was originally known as 'Precentor's Pleasure'.

This tradition has continued to this day, and the concert series has included a series of lunchtime recitals and an evening concert featuring local soloists and award-winners from the Countess of Munster scheme for young professional artists. In recent years, this concert has been organised and conducted by John Davenport, former Head of Music at Clifton College and an active member of the Bristol Cathedral Concerts Committee. Supporting young artists at the start of their career has become a feature of his programmes and recent highlights have included memorable performances of Mozart's Concerto for Flute and Harp, a spell-binding recital by violinist Julia Hwang, and appearances by Brett Baker, Richard Marshall and his wife Rebecca from the famous Black Dyke Band. There have also been a number of appearances by Bristol's own soprano, Josephine Goddard. Josephine became a firm favourite with audiences and later went on to sing in a rain-soaked but brilliant performance of 'Land of Hope of Glory' on live television during the regatta for the Queen's Jubilee in 2012.

93

CATHEDRAL PROCESSIONS

Cathedrals offer outstanding spaces for movement, and Bristol Cathedral is no exception. *A New Dictionary of Liturgy and Music* describes a procession as 'a planned movement of a group of people from one place to another for some specific religious purpose, often to the accompaniment of singing and music'. Processions stretch way back to the fourth century in Christendom, with a description of pilgrimages to the sacred sites in Jerusalem during the rites of Holy Week. In a sense, in whatever century they occur, processions will always help the people of God to act out their identity as pilgrims moving towards God. They invite us all on an interior spiritual journey as we reflect again on our own journey of faith.

The wonderful seasons of Advent, Epiphany, Candlemas, Holy Week and Easter are ideal times of year for using the whole space of the Cathedral as it was originally envisaged – that is, as a theatre for procession and pilgrimage. Mindful of the glorious acoustic of Bristol Cathedral and watching and listening to the singing of the Advent Prose as the choir processes from the Eastern Lady Chapel to the West End, one cannot fail to kindle expectant hope in the hearts of the congregation – 'From darkness to light'. And there is nothing so sublime as the procession into the Cathedral

Palm Sunday procession round College Green

from the Easter bonfire in the serene garden at dawn on an Easter morning. As daylight begins to grow, so the huge paschal candle leads a procession of choir, clergy and people into the darkness of the nave, lighting up every corner of this sacred space, as one by one all the little hand-held candles get lit. And all this happens in silence and with a simple plainsong sung by the Deacon, 'The Light of Christ', and answered by the people, 'Thanks be to God'.

The Friends of Bristol Cathedral is a registered charity which works together with the Cathedral Chapter to fund projects which beautify the Cathedral, care for its fabric and enrich its worship. The Friends feel a particular responsibility to help with projects which enhance the Cathedral or its life, but which it would be difficult for the Chapter to fund from within its normal financial resources. This has made an enormous difference to the musical life of the Cathedral over the years. In addition, one of their number, Lilian Simmons, left a specific legacy to the Music Department, and this

Grand piano purchased by the Friends. (DB)

is administered by the Trustees of the Friends. This fund has specifically helped out with the cost of soloists for concerts, new music and instrumentalists for special services.

Below are itemised some of the contributions made since 1971:

1971	£500	Towards the restoration of the organ
1975		Payment for four recordings made by the choir
1987	£200	For music
1988	£500	For music
1989		New psalters for the choir
1993	£600	Towards the Cathedral Music Library
1996	£36,000	Towards a new sound system
2000		Grand piano in memory of Clifford Harker
	£1300	Towards an anthem written by David Briggs: 'When in our music God is glorified', to celebrate the 10th Anniversary of the Girls' Choir
2008/9	£254	For a second hymn-book trolley
2013	£4,000	Towards the publication of *A History of the Music of Bristol Cathedral in 100 Objects*

In addition to the above, the Friends made a sizeable contribution towards the new Luke Hughes choir stalls, which match the nave altar that he had constructed.

THE SHIP'S BELL

In the south transept the bell of HM Aircraft Carrier *Argus* is hung, and it is struck three times to announce the beginning of a Eucharist or a large service. The commanding nature of this sound calls us all to order. Like all large ships' bells, it has an amazing capacity to cut through bustling preparation and the chatter of a gathering congregation; it is another example of ordered sound

The *Argus* bell in the South Transept. (DB)

helping us to focus our minds and hearts on the worship that is about to start.

HMS *Argus* started life as an Italian liner in 1914. Its hull was bought by the navy and was converted into an aircraft carrier in 1918. After that it served in conflicts all over the world:

Grand Fleet	1918-19
Atlantic Fleet	1919-25
Arctic	1941
Atlantic	1941-2
North Africa	1942
Malta Convoy	1942

The bell has been loaned to the Cathedral through the generosity of the Bristol Shiplovers' Society. The frame that supports the one-hundredweight bell was built by the Chairman of the Society and is dedicated to Canon Percival Gay, a well-known Bristol clergyman who was chaplain on the *Argus* from 1939 to 1943.

Architectural historian Sir Nikolaus Pevsner said that Bristol Cathedral 'has the saltiest history of any in England'. Its story is interwoven with that of a busy port served by the River Avon and linked to the Bristol Channel via the Severn. It is therefore very appropriate for the Cathedral to be summoned to our core responsibility of worship by this symbol of Bristol's maritime heritage.

'THE TRUTH SHALL SET YOU FREE'

On 25 March 2007 a special service took place in the Cathedral to commemorate the Act for the Abolition of the Slave Trade, which was passed exactly 200 years before, in 1807. Bristol Blue Glass Ltd donated a large blue-glass bowl for liturgical use in that service, and it has since become an appropriate 'font' for baptism.

The glass bowl has an inscription on it from which was drawn the title of a CD made by the Cathedral Choir and the Girls' Choir

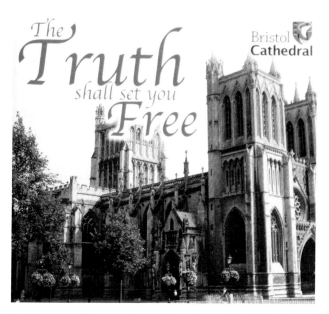

The Truth shall set you Free

Bristol Cathedral

during that year. The words are taken from John 8.32: '... and you will know the truth, and the truth will make you free' – the CD is entitled *The Truth Shall Set You Free*. The theme of liberation is one that is found at the very core of the Christian gospel, and it felt very appropriate to reflect on that truth in the choice of music and readings. The music therefore incorporates a great deal of Easter repertoire right through to an evocative arrangement of the Negro spiritual 'Deep River' from Michael Tippett's *A Child of Our Time*.

Mention must be made of the inclusion in the 25 March service of the newly formed University of the West of England Gospel Choir, conducted by Kim Samuels, which has since gone from strength to strength. With a large and historic black community in Bristol, the Cathedral has increasingly welcomed into its midst some outstanding gospel choirs, including a recently formed choir from the Cathedral Choir School. These have all considerably enhanced the variety of music on offer.

BRISTOL CHOIRBOOK — THE VISION

The Eton Choirbook gave us the idea. This book originally contained music by 24 different composers and is one of three large choirbooks surviving from early-Tudor England. What drew us to the concept was the proud sense of ownership that Eton College has over its manuscripts, and particularly over this centuries-old book. We thought it would be a good idea if Bristol Cathedral also had a choirbook that it could be proud of. It would contain contributions from Cathedral composers as well as current Chapter members. The idea was presented to Chapter and readily accepted. It soon became clear that this would also provide a seemly gift for the current Dean, the Very Rev. Robert Grimley, who was due to retire on Trinity Sunday 2009.

The Augustinian vision for the work and mission of the Abbey has been a constant inspiration for the people of Bristol Cathedral, and Dean Grimley had already collected a number of descriptions of the nature of that Augustinian community. Words such as these:

The Augustinians wanted to suffer weakness with the weak, and the distressed, and with the fallen. They wanted to be a light in a dark place 'For God, who commanded the light to shine out of darkness, hath shined in our hearts, to give the light of the knowledge of the glory of God in the face of Jesus Christ.'

Not only did they want their own members to abide by the values of community living, they also wanted to teach those values to others. And God said, 'let there be light: and there was light'.

They wanted to live with their fellow men and women in a way that led to more wholesome lives, and to the conversion of the wicked. But in a sense that meant that they would live as strangers, as well as neighbours. 'And God saw the light, that it was good: and God divided the light from the darkness. And God called the light Day, and the darkness he called Night. And the evening and the morning were the first day.'

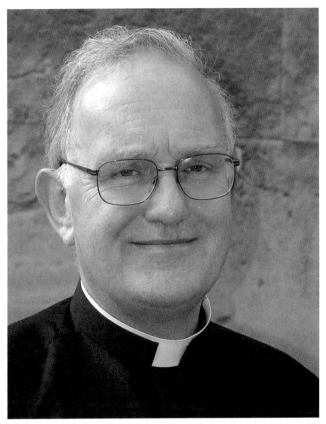

Very Revd. Robert Grimley

The five Cathedral composers took their inspiration not only from these words but also from different spaces in the building, and set about writing compositions. The writings were interspersed with these compositions and they were eventually bound together to create a Bristol Choirbook. Dean Grimley was proudly presented with the result on Trinity Sunday.

When the Dean, Chapter and Organist Mark Lee decided to pursue the idea of a new 'Bristol Choirbook' in which artistic and spiritual gifts might combine, the five composers set about their work in 2008/9.

As has been stated, the concept was to dedicate a new composition to a different space in the building, and the composers were encouraged to choose the physical space that most suited their musical vision. Philip Wilby composed a setting of George Herbert's 'Prayer', to be sung by male voices in the Eastern Lady Chapel. Paul Walton's 'Third Service' was written to be performed in the choir, and David Bednall's 'I am the Light of the World' was composed to be sung in the nave. Mark Lee provided a grace to be performed in the chapter house and Rob Waters, an alto Lay Clerk of the time, wrote a celebratory anthem to be performed on top of the Cathedral tower on the morning of Ascension Day. His setting of John Donne's 'Salute the last and everlasting day' is dedicated thus: 'An anthem for Ascension for the Singing men of Bristol Cathedral'. The whole set of pieces concluded with a triumphal descant by Paul Walton for the hymn tune 'Abbot's Leigh'.

Last verse arrangement

Saviour, if/since of Si-on's city I___through grace___ a mem-ber am,
Let___the world de-ride___ or pi-ty, I___will glo - ry in___ thy name:
Fa - ding is___ the world - ling's plea-sure, All___ his boast-ed pomp___ and show,
So - lid joys and last - ing trea-sure None___ but Si - on's chil - dren know.

187

As the tenth anniversary of the horrific events that befell New York drew closer, it was strongly felt by the Cathedral that the moment should not be allowed to pass unmarked. To this end the Bristol Cathedral Concert Choir mounted a performance of the Verdi Requiem with a choir of 160 volunteers, four soloists and the New Bristol Sinfonia. It was set up on one piano rehearsal in a local Bristol church, together with an orchestral rehearsal on the day.

A stunning performance ensued that drew admiration from the local press, who enthused about all aspects of the performance, not failing to notice the striking of the Cathedral clock at 9 pm, just as the final chord diminished. It was a most telling moment, which transplanted the music from the world of the concert hall to its full memorial and liturgical role.

Bristol Cathedral Concert Choir

new bristol sinfonia

Conductor: MARK LEE

TWIN TOWERS MEMORIAL
CHARITY CONCERT

VERDI
REQUIEM

NAOMI HARVEY - soprano
JOANNE THOMAS - mezzo
IAN YEMM - tenor
MARTIN LE POIDEVIN - bass

BRISTOL CATHEDRAL
SATURDAY 10 SEPTEMBER, 7.30pm
THIS EVENT IS OPEN TO ALL SINGERS
Up to a limit of 180
Rehearsals on
Thursday 8 September at 7.30pm and
Saturday 10 September at 2.00pm

All the musicians involved in this project are giving
their services free and all the profits will be donated to

THE FIRE FIGHTERS CHARITY
www.firefighterscharity.org.uk

TICKETS

SINGERS £5.00 - may be ordered using the form overleaf
AUDIENCE £5.00 - Available from:
Providence Music, 1 St Georges Rd, Bristol, BS1 5UL. 0117 927 6536
(Credit cards accepted)
They may also be ordered using the form overleaf which is also available on
our website www.concertchoir.co.uk

VISITORS' COMMENTS

Here are some comments about music and worship from the time of the Abbey:

> Visitation by Bishop Godfrey Giffard in 1278:
> … the house is not well ruled in temporal matter, for none of the brethren know what they have or what they are to spend. The canons were ordered not 'to fly out of the choir like bees' as soon as services were ended, but to remain and pray for their benefactors.

> Joseph Leech in 1845:
> … upon the whole I would be much impressed with Cathedral service, if the choristers would impart a little more decent solemnity to their demeanour, and not throw themselves irreverently about as though they would say 'we are paid for singing, but there was nothing about worshipping God in the agreement.'

Dean Pigou talks of an old apple-woman sitting at some steps facing the Cathedral who had no doubt been the victim of choirboys upsetting her basket of apples and oranges. You can hear her South-West accent as she comments: 'Ah! They thinks you cherabims and seraphims over there, but I knows better.'

More recently, in May 2012, a couple from Germany wrote an email:

> Two days ago we attended the Choral Evensong at the really spectacular Bristol Cathedral. We were very affected by the warm and friendly welcome, especially by one of the clergy members who took the time to speak with us at great length. It is good to know that church can appeal to visitors in that way. Unfortunately we're missing this impression in our home country Germany very often. The service itself and the music was really wonderful.

Contributors

Canon Wendy Wilby – editor and contributor.
Wendy was educated at Oxfod University followed
by the Royal College of Music. One of the first
women priests to be ordained in 1994, she moved
to Bristol with her composer husband, Philip, at
the end of 2006. As a member of the Chapter of
Bristol Cathedral and Precentor she heads up the
music and liturgy department and takes day-to-day
responsibility for all arrangements surrounding the
Cathedral's worship. She feels privileged to
occupy one of the most delightful jobs in the C of E.
(Objects 4, 6, 8, 13, 15, 18, 19, 26, 28, 31, 32, 37,
38, 40, 44, 48, 49, 51, 54, 58, 59, 60, 63, 66, 67, 68, 69, 75, 76, 78, 79, 80, 81,
85, 86, 88, 93, 94, 95, 96, 100)

Darren Bell is Head of Photography at Harrow School. He is responsible for
taking many of the images in this volume.

Dr Joseph Bettey has lectured and written many books on religious history,
church architecture and the study of local history. He was formerly Reader in
Local History at Bristol University. (Objects 47, 74)

Frank Clarke has worshipped at Bristol Cathedral for a number of years and is
a trained guide. (Objects 70, 71)

Mark Lee was educated at Cambridge University. He was appointed in 1998
as Director of Music, having spent eight years as Assistant Organist at
Gloucester Cathedral and two years on the music staff at Westminster School
prior to that. (Objects 9, 27, 50, 53, 99)

Patricia Morris has been a member of the Cathedral congregation for many
years and is now editor of the *Friends' Annual Report*. (Object 87)

Stephen Parsons is a passionate and committed Bristolian with a vision for
the city and its future. Educated and a chorister at Bristol Cathedral School, he
is now Chair of governors at BCCS (Bristol Cathedral Choir School) as well as
representing causes connected with charity, education and the elderly.
(Objects 33, 57, 82)

Gordon Pullin was a Choral Scholar at St John's College, Cambridge, and a member of the choirs of Coventry Cathedral (at the time of its consecration), York Minster and St Paul's. He has also been a frequent deputy in the cathedral choirs of Norwich, Chester, St Edmundsbury, Ely, St Alban's, Wells, Bristol, Westminster Abbey and Westminster Cathedral. (Objects 7, 29, 34, 36, 39, 42, 56, 83, 84)

Canon John Rogan is the Cathedral Archivist and served as a Canon Residentiary from 1979-89. He contributed to and edited the book *Bristol Cathedral: History and Architecture*. (Objects 1, 73)

Paul Walton began his musical career at Holy Trinity Church, Stratford-upon-Avon (Shakespeare's church) and is currently Assistant Organist at Bristol Cathedral. He is also active as a conductor and recitalist throughout the UK and abroad and recently recorded his first commercial CD. (Objects 10, 11, 12, 52)

Julian Warren is one of the archivists based at Bristol Record Office, where the archives of Bristol Cathedral are deposited. He was to a large extent responsible for 'Treasures in Store', an exhibition of Bristol Diocesan and Cathedral archival material on display during the spring of 2010. (Objects 2, 3, 21, 64, 65, 89)

Dr Philip Wilby is a composer and church musician. He was educated at Leeds Grammar School and Keble College, Oxford, and joined the staff at the University of Leeds in 1972, where eventually he became Professor of Composition. He now lives in Bristol with his wife, Wendy. (Objects 5, 14, 16, 17, 20, 22, 23, 24, 25, 30, 35, 41, 43, 55, 72, 90, 91, 92, 97, 98)